INSIDE THE MUSIC

INSIDE THE MUSIC

The Life Of Idris Muhammad

IDRIS MUHAMMAD

Library of Congress Control Number: 2012905772
ISBN: Hardcover   978-1-4691-9217-8
                 Softcover   978-1-4691-9216-1
                 Ebook   978-1-4691-9218-5

To order additional copies of this book, contact:
Xlibris Corporation
1-888-795-4274
www.Xlibris.com
Orders@Xlibris.com
112876

Contents

Section One—The Neighborhood

Section Two—Trouble

Section Three—Roots Of Rock 'n' Roll

Section Four—Early Days in NYC

Section Five—Introduction to Jazz Scene

Section Six—Hair

Section Seven—The Seventies

Section Eight—Today

Section One

The Neighborhood

Living Near the Mississippi River

As kids in New Orleans we didn't wear no shoes. Summertime was hot. When a hurricane come through it would blow the river and the water overflows its banks—it would flood—and that's when we'd go out there. Fishing poles, nets and baskets.

In order to get to the water you had to step in the mud. And that mud would be all over your feet. The river water was muddy. My mother didn't allow us in the river because it was too dangerous.

Nice big frogs, crab, crawfish, shrimp, get a sack of that stuff. We'd go get a whole basketful and bring that back home. People would see you with that basket of big old fish. Sell some of that on the way back home! You'd eat good that night. That's what we used to do.

And if you swam in the river, then as you walked back from the river to where we lived, the sun dried your ass off—all you had to do was take your nails and scratch your skin—wasn't nothing but mud.

Your mama says, "You been out in that river?"

"No ma'am."

So your mother knew you was in the river and she'd beat the tar out of you because cats drowned out there. Playing all day without a shirt on and no shoes, trousers rolled up at the knee, that night I might get an asthma attack. We were told we couldn't go near the river.

Barefoot at the waterfront, the river looks like a solid piece of earth moving in reverse. Catch the water in a certain way and it looks like you can walk right out over surface of it. The waves come in, and then the waves retreat because the water has to go out. The river has a mysterious way of moving yet not moving. And it was muddy, muddy waters, man.

We live right down the street from the Mississippi River.

Dr. Wilson's Yard

Dr. Wilson was the black doctor in our neighborhood. He had a beautiful house set inside a white picket fence. Inside this great big yard he had a whole orchard of different fruits. His family would never eat them so we'd go down to Dr. Wilson's house, jump over the picket fence and we'd steal his fruits from his trees. All different kinds of fruit trees. Then go jump back over the fence and eat them on the way down to the Neville's house. Every day my mother would say, "Don't go into Dr. Wilson's yard."

Getting over that picket fence was a big problem. Because I was short, it would come way up over the top of my head. Trying to climb over it, I always got my pants caught in the pickets. It would tear my pants. And then, after you get into the yard, then you got to get back over the fence to get out. Man, it looked like that fence was ten feet tall. You don't want to go out through the front door.

Now you got figs and you got apples, peaches, pears—all this fruit in your pockets. And as you're trying to get over the fence, some of this fruit is bustin' open in your pockets.

We'd get to Arthur Neville's house and his dad would say, "What you all been doin'?"

And we'd say, "Well, we ain't be doin' nothin', Mr. Neville . . . we ain't be doin' nothin'."

And he'd say, "What's the matter with your hands then?"

We'd be like, "What hands . . . there's nothin'."

"That color. Where is that color from?"

And it was from the pomegranate. The dye from the pomegranate. It was all in your hands—in between your fingers—and you got the seeds from the figs, they're smashed in between your fingers and he'd say but what is that? And he knew we'd been in Dr. Wilson's yard. And we ain't supposed to go in there. And your mama, she'd wash your clothes and she sees the figs, sees the pears and the skins and beats your ass. Get an ass whippin'.

Your mama says, "You been over to Dr. Wilson's yard?"

"No ma'am." I'd tell my mama it was the flavoring from an Italian Ice. "It was a Sno-ball," I'd say.

And then she washed my pants and she sees the skins in my pockets, juice down my shirt, pants torn where it catch on the picket fence. Now I got to figure out how to tell my mama how I torn my pants.

But Dr. Wilson, he didn't mind us taking his fruits because his family wasn't eating all of that stuff. But our family was stealing. And they didn't want us to steal. Dr. Wilson didn't really care that we were taking it because it would just fall on the ground and rot anyhow.

Behind the Mask

The only horses we had was a broomstick. We would go to the place where they killed the chickens in the market and we would get the feathers from the chickens. Some would be Indians. Some would be cowboys. We put the chicken tail feathers on the Indians.

The Indians would shoot at the cowboys, the cowboys would shoot at the Indians, lasso the bad guys, round them up and put them in jail. There were boxcars by the railroad tracks. We weren't allowed to go near the rail yard because it was too dangerous. So we'd drag the guys who would be captured down to the railroad tracks and put them in the boxcars.

Or we would put them in a certain area of someone's yard and wrap a chain-link fence around them. We built a jail out of chain-link fence and put the prisoners inside of it. That was the jail. After the jail would be full we'd let all the cats out or we wouldn't have nobody to play with.

Tom Mix—who was the famous cowboy at that time—he was my idol. I had some jeans and a cowboy shirt and a cowboy hat and a cowboy mask so I'd be a cowboy on Mardi Gras Day. Ever since I was a small kid I always wanted to be the cowboy.

The mask is to disguise people who want to have a good time, drink a lot, maybe they'd go grab somebody's backside. If somebody did something to you during that year, you weren't able to get them back, and then you'd try to catch them on Mardi Gras Day. Do something to them where they don't know who did it. A guy would beat up a guy and have a clown suit on. Or he might be dressed like the Lone Ranger.

And when they'd say, "Who did it?"

"The guy who had the Lone Ranger mask on."

So they used to go down to the corner, take off the mask, and put another one on. It was kind of like that. I used to put on the mask.

But my mother had a saying, "I know who you are, Mardi Gras."

So, in other words, she'd say to the person behind the mask, I know who you are with that mask on. I know who you are, Mardi Gras.

Levi's

Jeans was a thing that you wore around Mardi Gras time. Western cats wore them in Texas and Arizona. It was working-people trousers and low-life trousers. It wasn't had no class to it. We only wore them at Mardi Gras time because only jeans could stand the Mardi Gras day wear and tear. You'd be on your knees trying to get the beads or climbing up the trees and only Levi's could take that wear.

When you bought a new pair of Levi's them boys was so stiff you would get cuts in your ankle and it hurt. So then my mama used to buy them long so we rolled 'em up above the ankle. But then you'd have welts in the crease of your knee—where they'd rub up against your skin—that'd be all raw right down in that crease.

Nobody ever thought of washing them before you wear them. You just put them on new. They was like boards. You had to wear them boys awhile. Didn't nobody think they got softer after you washed them. But brand new? Man, oh man. Didn't nobody think. We just put them on new. We used to play cowboys and Indians in the French Market. And Levi's was for cowboys.

Fishing Poles

Can you see that streetcar coming down the tracks? That's the St. Charles Line, man. New Orleans is known for its streetcars. I used to ride the St. Charles line with my mother to go uptown. But I preferred to travel that same line downtown with my father with our fishing poles and our bags. It was a twenty minute ride on the St. Charles Line to the lake where we would fish.

My dad would explain to me on the ride how we was surrounded by the Gulf of Mexico, Lake Pontchartrain and the Mississippi River.

"You got ocean, lake and river. So there's three beds of water. That's why the fishing is so good."

We made our own nets, bags and fishing poles. My dad showed me how to do this. Cut through the bamboo pole and take it apart at the joints; brush shellac over the pieces and let them dry. Now you can slide one piece down inside the other. Then wrap this peculiar-looking fishing wire around it and you've got a bamboo fishing pole. My dad would build fishing poles like this out of a single piece of bamboo.

Then my dad made a bag for it which kind of looked like a pool bag—you know how the cats would carry their pool stick in a bag—so we had the fishing poles in this special-made cloth bag. To top it off, my daddy even made the container to hold the fish. To make it waterproof, he would sew together a bag made out of a raincoat. Sew the liner into the inside so that it wouldn't drip when you had wet fish down in there.

When we come to the lake we take the poles out of the bag, put them together, put the line on it, put the weight, bait it with the hook, throw it in the water. Splash!

That particular streetcar, the St. Charles Line, runs next to the graveyard and across the street from the field where we used to run around, play baseball and all kinds of sports. We had neighborhood football games on that field in the fall and winter when it got cooler. Surrounded by water, it would get cold outside and the water would get cold and make the dampness. But it never would freeze.

We played football in the cold dampness on that field. You be hit so very nice; hit you good, man. Talk about hitting you, man—*ooh wee*—guys would knock teeth out. Guys used to get their ass busted. I loved to play football. Knock the bejesus out of you.

Catholic Church and Catholic School

There is a Catholic church off Magazine Street where we used to go with my mother. Come out of the house Sunday morning and take her hand and walk to church. Down the block, these bony black dogs would lurch at us; they would rush the black wrought iron gates and chicken-wire fences.

We'd get to the church and the pastor would be standing there, holding open the huge carved and paneled double doors. Inside, the mass was kind of quiet. It was peaceful. There was a life-size crucifix up front that I used to stare at.

"How long has he been up there like that?" I asked.

"A long time."

"He's God? He can do anything? Can He turn His head to the other side?"

My mama pinched the shit out of me because you can't hit them in church you know. She used to have a way where she'll grab your skin and twist it into a knot. She grabbed me and she pinched me with that twist.

I'm a kid so I don't know that it was made out of plastic, mud and clay. Since He's God, I thought, can He do anything? Can He turn his head to the other side? I got scolded by that. But I was inquisitive about God even then.

I was originally enrolled in the Catholic school. But the nuns used to beat us so bad that I knew there wasn't no God in their hearts. They beat your ass so bad, man. I'm doing something I'm not supposed to be doing. So they'd make you put your hand out. They'd take the ruler and they'd hit you in the hand.

Once I did something and when the nun raised up to hit me I moved my hand out of the way. The nun hit her own leg because I had moved my hand so fast. Because my hand was hurting so bad I couldn't take it no more. She starts coming down—I moved my hand out—and whap! She hit her own leg.

She whipped my ass so bad I had welts on me. Beat the shit out of me. In those days the nuns used to have their heads shaved. Or they'd cut if off real close to the scalp.

I told her if she hit me again, "I'll take that hat,"—you know, they used to wear that wimple hat, which is part of their habit—"and I'll snatch it right off your bald head."

She beat my ass real good. Beat the shit out of me. Beat my ass good.

Shoeshine on Magazine Street

I had a shoebox that my dad made for me and I had shoe polish and the rags and the brushes. I used to go down to Magazine Street because they had quite a few bars there—mostly white bars—and I would go in these bars and ask the guys:

"Anybody want a shoeshine?"

They'd say, "Yeah, come on in."

I'd shine one guy's shoes and the guys would say, "Your shoes look good. Shine mine." And I'd end up with about four or five shoeshines. Four or five shoeshines at a crack!

My mother used to be angry. "Don't you ever go in that bar again. I don't want you on Magazine Street anymore. I don't like that."

I'd tell her what went down and there were certain things she didn't like. Because the white guys used to tell me when I was down on my knees shining their shoes, "I'll give you fifty cents if you let me rub your hair."

"I'll give you fifty cents," because they used to say that if you rub a black kid's head it would give you good luck. I'd come out with about close to two dollars. That was one of my first jobs.

So I'd say, "Give me the fifty cents!"

That started everything for me. I made a killing at that. As far as trying to make money to go to the movies and trying to do things, little hustles, I always knew how to make money. I'm making beer deliveries and racking pool balls by night.

By day, old ladies coming from the grocery store—carrying three or four bags and needing help getting their groceries home—I'd carry their groceries to the big houses on Napoleon Avenue and St. Charles Street. Clean people's swimming pools. Cut their grass and take the leaves out. Clean the rose gardens of the ladies in this neighborhood.

After the chores and hustles were done, I can remember walking to the Neville's house, just around the corner and down Valence Street. Maybe run into somebody we could heckle, steal some plums out of Dr. Wilson's yard.

Streetcars, Graveyards and Football Practice

Albert and Papa, these were two brothers who lived in the neighborhood. They had big helmet heads, what we used to call water-heads. They were tough and they could fight, man. Oh god, they were tough. You got in a fight with Albert then you had to fight his brother too. You don't want to fight these cats because they'd kick your ass, man.

Albert and Papa were the only two cats in the neighborhood that I couldn't beat. So we were friends. The baddest cats in the neighborhood, they were my buddies. I knew these guys from when we were in kindergarten and up. We'd play football until it got dark and we'd all run home.

You have your uniform and your gear on, and you're coming from practice and you've got these cleats—you know the metal spikes that they used to have—and as you go through the graveyard at nighttime you hear: Clack . . . clack . . . clack . . . clack—with the football shoes on. And all of a sudden one cat starts to break out and running and clack . . . clack . . . clack . . . clack. Then he starts to running faster: Click, click, click, click, click and you don't see him no more.

*   *   *

I'm going to tell you something about New Orleans and the burial system in New Orleans. Why do they have the burial houses above ground? The reason why they bury above the ground is because this is all swampland. Because this is all swamp, the ground is still sinking.

So they put tombs up above the ground. One tomb could house two people: one on the top, one on the bottom. That big one right there is about eight people, whole family.

We have a plot, but it's the whole family plot. Whoever died next would go in there.

*   *   *

Now the cat in the cleats, he done hid down behind a tree, now he done hid behind one of the graveyard tombs. And then you're walking—you didn't see him hiding, right—some kid would just be afoot. A guy would jump out and scream 'Bahhh!' and we would all break out and runnin'.

Guys would run over cats with their metal cleats. One time, as I made a run for it, a dog started out to chasing me and it bit me on my leg. They had to carry the dog and me to the hospital.

For three days, they're checking me and the dog for any signs of rabies. We didn't have a car to bring the dog in so the next thing it was on the St. Charles streetcar line. Now we got a dog in a box.

My daddy killed it, see. The dog bit me and my daddy killed it graveyard dead. So when I went to the hospital they said you had to bring the dog in a box to check it for rabies. Paper all wrapped around it, pine oil and camphor balls so it didn't stink.

After three days my mother said, "No more of this here. Put the dog up." That day we threw the dog in the garbage can.

I can remember running through that graveyard at dusk after football practice—scare the shit out of each other, hide behind the tombs and like that—because it was something to do for excitement. On the way home, we might race down the street with our cleats on to the bakery on Prytania Street or the candy store on Lyons.

You can hear us coming on.

Candy Store

The candy store sells everything. It looks like a house. The only thing that shows it isn't a house is the plate glass window facing Lyons Street with black and gold cursive letters that reads: Candy Shop.

"Hey Leo," the guys would say. "Tell him you want five cents of them candies up there on the shelf."

We used to go over there and buy some candies and make him turn his back to us. The only problem is, the owner's got a small series of glass cases and a thin mirror strip set up above the shelves. When he turns his back on you to reach for something, he can see everything happening in his store. We don't know he can see us so we commence to shoveling candies in our pockets—not knowing he's watching us with the glass and the mirror.

He's watching kids coming and going through the front door, kids stealing from him—everything. He just lets us take it. And then when your mama would come to get something for the family, he'd say to her such an amount of candies was stolen the other day.

So the mother would pay him. And whip your ass. I got busted like that once.

"This is what's going to happen to you when you're stealing." And my mother took my hand and she put it into the fire and burned the tips of my fingers. "The devil will take you to hell. You're going to burn," she'd say.

She burned my fingertips—burned the shit out of me—my whole fingers and hands were hurting, too. But stealing was a mischievous thing and there was an ass whippin' for it—just like going into Dr. Wilson's yard. We'd get busted and not even realize what we were doing.

Because we had so much of the peaches and stuff, being on your fingers, on your clothes—you been eating them, juice all down your shirt, playing in the grass and it's got grass on your pants, figs in your pocket and it'd pop—the seeds of the figs in your pockets would pop open. And when my mama washed the pants and washed the shirts—oh man—we just busted ourselves.

But Dr. Wilson, he didn't mind us taking his fruits because his family wasn't eating all of that stuff. Sometimes he'd just leave the gate unlocked so you could just walk in the yard and take anything you want, pears on the ground. He didn't care who jumped over and took some of that stuff. He didn't give a damn. And it was kind of like that at the candy store. The candy store would just let you walk right out with your pockets full of candies. That was a part of us, part of growing up in our neighborhood.

It was clean. It was innocent. My mama was trying to teach us the right way to go. On the one hand, I always had my chores with my mama, but on the other hand, I was always prone to commit some mischief.

Railroad Tracks and Shotgun Houses

I go with my mother to the railroad tracks in the wintertime. Workers load the boxcars with coal using a big crane. As they drop the coal into the boxcars—the boxcars are brimming with coal, all this coal spilling over onto the tracks—my mother and I would approach the tracks at night and pick up that spilled coal.

Our house was six blocks north of the riverfront. The railroad tracks, the cranes, the coal and the men with shovels were at Tchoupitoulas Street. We'd bring those sacks of coal back to the house at 4915 Coliseum Street.

My brother's job was to clean those fireplaces out every morning. In the evening, I would come from school, take that coal and add wood and kerosene and paper so everything would be ready to make a fire when my dad came home from work. That's the only heating that we had. The way New Orleans houses are, this house has a fireplace in every room. We'd light these fires to warm the house. Wintertime, the house smelled of wood smoke.

We lived in a straight-through house—what they called a shotgun house—that originally had four rooms. The term shotgun means that you could stand at the front door and fire a shotgun straight through and it would come out the back door without hitting anything.

Others say it is because the rooms of the house are divided on two sides, like two barrels of a shotgun. Either way is correct. It was the style of architecture in New Orleans because that's how the people made their homes in West Africa. When these original people settled in New Orleans they brought this construction with them.

My dad was a builder and interior designer. He would do all the work himself on the house. If something happened to the roof—if a storm would come through—then my dad would repair it. As the family would grow he would add rooms onto the house. We ended up with six rooms. But we didn't have a washroom—the family used to bathe with a metal tub. It was the only washroom we had was a metal tub.

Come to find out the people who sold us the house didn't sell us the full mortgage. There was another mortgage on that house besides the one that we had. And the new owners—who we ended up renting from—they put us out. That's how we'd end up living right around the corner at 1220 Lyons Street

There was a mysterious fire at 1220 Lyons Street.

1220 Lyons Street

The original location of Buddy's Cleaners and Pressing Shop, 1220 Lyons Street, is made of wood and has a single residence upstairs. The upstairs tenant runs an underground business out of his home up there above the cleaning shop.

They might gamble up there. Roll dice. Play cards. 1220 Lyons Street is a full-blown gaming establishment where all the guys would go after the bars are closed at night. There was a fire there and it burned the whole place down. It burned it down, man.

So after the fire, the Buddys rebuilt their cleaning business out of cement blocks on just the street level and they split from the building to a separate residence in the same neighborhood. We call Mrs. Buddy "Ms. Nermy," which is short for her first name, Minerva.

The Buddys moved into a big house just around the corner on Coliseum Street. Coliseum Street, Upper Line Street and Lyons Street form a triangle—the French Square. It's a three-sided Square.

The front of the building is a restaurant and a pool hall. This new concrete structure, the rebuilt Buddy's Cleaners standing at 1220 Lyons Street, has apartment houses at either end, and around the backside. After it burned down and was rebuilt, that's when we took residency into an apartment at 1220 Lyons Street.

My sister Marilyn has the apartment on one side of Buddy's. We're on the other side. And my auntie Marie and her son—that's my cousin, known in the family as Uncle Leo—are on down the street from me. Further on down the street is where Ms. Booze lives. I say down the street, but these apartments are attached, like a Spanish compound. Ms. Booze loves her roses and she has a rose garden beneath her windows.

Our apartment is only three rooms: the living room and two bedrooms, plus a kitchen and now we have built-in bathroom. We have my mother and my father in one room. In the other bedroom, it's my nephew Henry and my brothers Frank and Sydney and me. So it's the four boys in that one room.

We sleep in a series of twin bunk beds stacked up against the walls. One sleeps with his head one way, and the other one sleeps with his head the other way. I bunked in the bed above my little brother Frank. And my brother Sydney slept below my nephew Henry.

These apartments are attached to the bar and the pool hall where the guys are playing Nine Ball and drinking beer, so we can hear their music coming in through the walls. We hear that all day and all night. Do you know how much music is in this neighborhood?

At night I'm making beer deliveries out the backside window of The Hole in the Wall tavern. Rack balls for my brother-in-law. Rack balls for the pool sharks playing Nine Ball. Deliver a cold glass of beer to Ms. Booze for a nickel. Making beer deliveries is one of my first money-making hustles.

This is after the Nevilles have moved into the neighborhood. The same age, Aaron Neville and I would just be walking down the street, singing. We don't have a care in the world. The only people who believe in us are our parents. The Neville's mother knew Aaron is going to do something. My folks aren't so sure.

My brother Sydney goes to work at the pharmacy and I come home from school and—oh man, after my chores is done—I play the shit out his drums. We always have drums set up in the living room against a window facing the street. This is when I began to practice on my brother Sydney's drums.

Peeing on Ms. Booze's Roses

"We'll give you a nickel if you pee on Ms. Booze's roses," they said.

"Yes sir, that's easy money," I told them. Give me that nickel."

I pulled ol' one eye out and started spraying Ms. Booze's roses when her window opened up. Oh god—I can't stop because the pee is all going up in the air and you can't stop.

She said, "You little nasty thing. I'm going to tell your mother. Put your thing up."

And you can't stop because once you start you can't stop. So finally you stop and put it up and before you could get home your mother's standing on the steps waiting for you. I got a good one that time. I was warned. My daddy warned me.

"You ever take that thing out in the street again I'll cut it off."

That's how mischievous I was. But I got a nickel. I got a hell of an ass-whipping for that nickel, yes sir. And everybody in the neighborhood, when I passed, it was:

"I don't believe he did that."

"That one right there?"

"Which one?"

"That one right there? That's Leo. Come here, boy."

"Leo, what made you do something like that?"

And they would drum it into your head.

"Your mama whip your ass, didn't she?"

"Yes ma'am."

"She should have whipped your little ragged ass. Go on about your business."

I'd get to the next corner and it was:

"Yeah, I heard about you peeing on . . ."

"Pee on my flowers!"

"Pee on mine! Look!"

And she had a broomstick right by the window.

"I got this broomstick just for your ass. Pee on my flowers! I'm going to whop you in the head with this here broomstick."

Shit man, I couldn't do nothin'. Everybody knew it.

That night, my dad and his buddies were in the beer parlor called The Hole in the Wall. I could hear them walking home, and they was laughing, they was laughing—and they asked my dad, they called my daddy Muz:

"Muz, did Leo do that?"

Dad said, "Yes."

"Somebody should have pissed on her flowers."

"Cause she ain't nothing but a door popper."

"She ain't going about her business."

"I'm sure glad somebody pissed on her flowers."

They had a good laugh. Later that night I hear my daddy telling this to my mama. They thought I was outdoors but I was in bed pretending to be sleeping.

After that you just want to lie down. Don't want to go outside because the cats see the marks on your ass, they know they done tore your ass up. Plus, your mother wouldn't let you go outside. You was punished—couldn't go outside—and hearing them laughing, my daddy telling my mama.

"The guys said they had the best laugh!"

"And Leo was peeing? Did he get all of them? How was he doing it?"

It was funny to them. But I only got a nickel. That's all I got. Two Tootsie Rolls for a penny, maybe get two Hershey's Kisses for a penny and three or four jelly beans for a penny—for a nickel you could get a lot of candies. And a hell of an ass-whipping.

McDonald #6

The schoolyard, which surrounds the red brick fortress at the corner of Lyons and Coliseum streets, is right across the street from our house. I'm late every day to school. I watch and I wait. When it's the last kid down in the schoolyard that's when I bolt across the playground and through the front doors at McDonald #6. And every day the principal is watching and he's waiting for me at the front door.

"Okay Morris, go up to the office."

Every day, every day, every day. I didn't like marching in the school yard. So I would be late for school every day. Every morning the whole school gathers in the main auditorium. The teachers walk through and collect all the kids from each grade and take us to our classrooms. That's where I met my first music teacher.

Mr. Solomon Spencer is the music teacher for all my brothers and sisters, cousins—everyone in the neighborhood. He had already instructed my oldest brother Weedy for twelve years. Plus, when I started school at six years old, my older brother Sydney was in the band when I got there.

The first day at McDonald #6, Mr. Spencer takes one look at me.

"Are you a Morris?"

"Yes sir. My name is Leo Morris."

"Follow me to the band room."

I didn't say a word.

Then he points and says, "Here's the drum."

Now we had to buy another school band uniform, which my mother didn't like because we didn't have the money. But the band looked sharp all uniformly dressed. Black shirts, black pants and white neckties. My mother tied the Windsor knot because I don't have no idea how to knot a necktie. So my mother helps me with this.

My family doesn't have the money for cymbal cleaner so my mom thinks if I made a mud pie and put it on the cymbal it would shine the cymbal without taking the metal off. How did we do that?

We take fresh dirt, mix it with water, and make some mud. Put this brown mud mixture on a clean white towel. Since the mud has got real fine silt and tiny pieces of sand in it, this will help pull the dirt out of the grooves of the cymbal—not polishing the cymbal, per se, just pulling away the grime.

So I discovered how to clean the cymbals with mud, dirt and rags from my mother. Because people don't have no money for school uniforms and cymbal polish and so forth, you learn how to be industrious.

Beer in a Bathtub

Early in the morning the people go out to the French Market and they buy a bushel of fish. Take it home, clean all the fish, and they ice it up. Then we get some chicken and do the same thing, clean the chicken, fry it Saturday night. Now we've got nice fried fish, fried chicken, some potato salad and some green peas, lettuce and tomato, piece of bread.

If somebody gets in jail then to make enough bail money to get them out somebody would have a supper for them. All their families are hustling to get the money to get the food. Or if the rent is due and they ain't got no money—the rent might be overdue two months—a good house party will make enough money to pay two months' rent.

We have nice cold beer in these bathtubs. Same tubs you might take a bath in the night before—people would bathe in these tubs—we have about five of those. Put all the sodas in one. Then put all the beers in the other. Take a fifty-pound block of ice, it would fill up two tubs. We had five of those tubs so that's two-, three-hundred pounds of ice I had to carry.

Take the front room and put the jukebox in it. It was only the songs that the person at that party likes. Next room, take the furniture out of that one and put it in the third room. Now you've got two rooms filled with people dancing. You just press a button and dance. Lord have mercy, guys dancing with the ladies.

String some lights up outdoors, put tablecloths out there on folding tables—the ones you fold down, the legs come out—and then the lady who owns the supper puts a dollar in the jukebox. It's a nickel a shot. We've got some music at a nickel a tune. Then we have people outside in the yard. We're having a party.

And a guy says, "Hey man, give me two beers."

The bottom layer of the tub would be covered in ice—beers jammed all down in there. Then another layer of ice, another layer of beers, and so on to the top layer—floating around on top of that ice—it was covered full of beers.

He gives me a nickel or a dime. Jax's, Regal, Falstaff and Dixie Beer—it was southern-brewed beers in New Orleans. And I'd reach in; give him two cold Jax's. When the beers go down, put more ice, more beers; fill these big round tin tubs with beers. That was my job.

Seventy-five cents for the supper, quarter for their beers, nickel for the jukebox, they had all the money to get the guy out on Sunday. And by the time the supper ended, as a young hustler icing the beer up, I'd have me a pocket full of money and I'd be in the corner sleeping, man. Make four or five dollars that night. Oh man, *that's* what New Orleans is about.

The French Market

You got crazy in McKenzie Bakery. You'd see all these lovely pastries and all kinds of cakes and pies and cookies and you wanted to buy everything but you didn't have no money. My auntie worked as a cashier at this bakery on Prytania Street. In the evenings after the stores closed, whatever wasn't sold that day in McKenzie's she took home with her. She gave us all kinds of pastries until we had too much on us.

My mother made all different kinds of food for us. She was a great cook. My mother was the chef in an Italian restaurant. I would walk to the French Market with my mother. We used to buy our produce, meats and poultry there. Outside, live chickens would be running wild in the street—running for their lives from the butcher. Fresh fish, rabbit, turtle, live chickens, they had everything you needed.

There was one guy in our neighborhood who had about ten children and he might need some help. So my mother would make a bag and we'd bring it to this guy's house. When you didn't have something and you needed that ingredient you could go to the neighbors and if they had it they would give it to you. It was that friendly of a neighborhood where you could share things.

Cup of sugar, cup of flour, some eggs—whatever you needed to make something with—you could just go through the neighborhood. My mother sent me many times to do this. So the people in the neighborhood would always bring something by the house in return.

I can't remember one day in my life going hungry. Every day I had something to eat. It might not have been what I wanted to eat, but we had food because we were sharing like that in the neighborhood.

The 13th Ward was full of people that had kids. People were kind. They were friendly. They were families. Our neighborhood was mostly musicians and schoolteachers.

Down the street from our house was a Baptist Church. On Sundays, you could hear the people playing the tambourines, singing songs and all like that in the Baptist church. This was in the French Market area—not the French Quarters. In the French Quarters you had voodoo and all this crazy shit.

My mother said, "Don't listen to that Voodoo. It's all in the brain."

It was there, though, because it could take hold in the mind. It's in the mind more than it is in the brain. And she didn't want somebody hung up with some voodoo shit.

Two Tribes

We had two Indian tribes in our neighborhood. Donald Harrison's father, who worked as the custodian of our elementary school, lived in the house adjacent to McDonald #6. Donald Harrison, Sr. was the chief of all the Indians in our neighborhood. His tribe was Guardians of the Flame.

Then we had Uncle Jolly. He was the chief a couple of blocks down. His tribe was the Wild Tchoupitoulas. These were the two Indian tribes in our neighborhood.

During the month of Mardi Gras, guys would start playing in their houses, and then they would come outside and play in the streets. It's called a dry run. They would go from bar to bar. And they would pull people out of each bar and lead them inside the next one. This was inside the square in the French Market. They would just second line down the streets and back to their houses.

On Mardi Gras day there are parades from morning until night. As the parade would second line, that bass drum attracted me because it was so big and loud. The bass drum player has got a cymbal turned upward on top of the bass drum. There's a coat hanger wrapped in a circle and stuffed down on a broom handle that's been cut off.

I would get underneath the bass drum as the band would come by and I would dance to it. *I was that small!* And the bass drum guy would say:

"Move your ass away from here before I hit you with this mallet."

Then I'd walk on the side of him and look at the people. There are some unusual costumes and you can tell by looking at the people, how they interact, what tribe they belong to. There's a ritual to it.

We used to wait on the corner of Coliseum and Lyons Street for the Indians to come out on Mardi Gras Day. Just a hundred and fifty steps from Dr. Wilson's yard, this is where it all started for me with the Indians.

There's a thrill of being inside a parade. I got a taste of that walking underneath the bass drum. You have to be in it to feel what is happening.

Spy Boy, Flag Boy, Big Chief

We have a Spy Boy, we have a Flag Boy, and we have a Chief.

Now the Spy Boy, as you know if you watch western movies, you know the Spy Boy is the guy who they send out and he's looking over the trees or he's looking off of his horse or he's looking behind a rock. The Spy Boy is in the front. He gives a signal to the Flag Boy. That's the Spy Boy.

Now the Flag Boy is the guy who lights the fire, puts the blanket over the fire, and makes the smoke. He's got the flag, and he's telling the Chief which tribe is coming. That's the Flag Boy. We're sending signals from the Spy Boy to the Flag Boy to the Chief.

So the Chief says, "Okay. Let's go get 'em."

And now we start to walk towards this tribe and the song they sing is: "Let's go get 'em. Let's go get 'em." So we're going to go meet this tribe. So this is basic of how the Indians run down in New Orleans. That's the rotation of how the tribe runs.

Now our tribe—we call it a gang—our gang, when we travel, we have a Spy Boy about a block ahead of us. Then we have a Flag Boy that's a half a block behind. And when the Spy Boy sees a guy coming he does a certain type of dance and points in this direction to say that the tribe is coming from this way.

First Job—Mardi Gras Parade

It's funny how things happened at this time. All my brothers played the drums. If you needed a drummer you'd go to the Morris House. My older brother Sydney had his drum set in the house so I saw how he did it. But I had never really played with a band before.

One Mardi Gras Day there was a knock on the door and it was all these old Dixieland musicians. They came looking for a drummer but all my brothers were already out working.

My mother answers the door and this guy spots me standing behind my mother. I was this itty-bitty little guy. They begged my mother and said they'd take care of me because I'm just eight or nine years old. So she made me go with them to the Mardi Gras Day Parade.

There's a truck parade and there's a float parade.

The truck parade starts on Napoleon Avenue at the intersection of Prytania Street. Prytania Street divides the white neighborhood from the black neighborhood. It goes past McKenzie Bakery and continues down Prytania Street and all the way downtown. I can see what's happening because they stacked beer cases for me to sit on and they put me on the back of a flatbed truck.

The first tune, "Bourbon Street Parade"—this particular tune has a drum intro and, oh man, I was playing! They had a big bass drum with a light inside that, every time you hit the bass drum, the light came on. They had the snare drum and one cymbal.

I knew the songs so it was easy to play. It was just the bass drum, the snare drum and the cymbal. So that wasn't hard. The guys really didn't care. They just wanted someone to keep time, somebody to make the big boom.

I'm inside the parade, riding on this nice decorated float. I'm seeing all my friends from school. I see this girl that I had been pulling her pigtails—her setting in front of me at school—she didn't like me so she used to embarrass me sometimes.

"Don't talk to me. That shirt that you got on, your brother wore it three days ago."

So I thought, *Okay, fine. It's like that.* She would come to school every day, all pressed and ironed. Now she sees me while I'm playing in the parade. She was surprised.

"Hey, Leo!" She was waving and yelling up at me. "Leo, Leo, Leo."

Mardi Gras Parade—Part Two

The music, the trinkets, the bands, the people, the costumes, all of this adrenaline is pumping. And her watching me, she's with her mother and father and family, perhaps she's saying to her mother, "This guy is my classmate, and he's on the float playing with the band. And he might look like a midget up there. How did he get up there?"

As she met the float, I said, "Hey baby, what's up?" And I thought, *okay, solid*. I was playing with her because she was surprised. And, in truth, I was surprised.

There are many, many people on the sidewalks—three, six, eight people deep from the curb—watching the trucks go by. The guys on the truck are throwing this stuff to the kids and the kids are trying to catch that stuff. And all the school kids—everybody in the neighborhood—is watching the parade, trying to catch beads or a trinket. Maybe catch a grasshopper or a frog, anything.

You can see the kids are shocked as they catch a pair of beads.

They ain't nothing but plastic beads and glass. Even though it wasn't thrown to you—it was just thrown to where you were standing, and you just put your hand up and they throw it right in your hand—but you put it over your neck and you wear it because you caught it.

Every dad wants to catch the best beads. The mother only wants the nice ones. So when he catches a cheap string of beads he puts them on his daughter. She might have so many beads you can't see her hair. The kids, they don't care, just give them beads.

When we finished the leader was passing out money. I'm just three feet tall, the guys all looking down at me, the leader scrapes together two five-dollar bills and hands them to me.

I had to ask him, "Do you get paid for doing this?" Because I had so much fun, and they slipped me a little wine and I had nice things to eat.

And he said, "Yes, of course. What did you think—we did this for nothing?"

The parade had begun at noon and by four o'clock my run was finished. By the end of the day they was all ripped.

Mardi Gras Parade—Part Three

The icing on the cake was seeing all my friends and seeing that girl. The cherry on the icing, though, is that I played with these old guys—and they seemed to think that I did it real well.

When we reached downtown, the people on the truck disbanded; they began heading to their parties. They was drunk. They was trying to figure out where the truck had stopped. Which way is home? But I know which way is home for me. All I have to do is to follow the truck route backwards to get straight back home.

I've got two five-dollar bills in my pocket and I'm not going to get on the streetcar and pay no six cents out of these five-dollar bills. The streetcar conductor, he's not going to change no five dollar bill anyway, so I walk home. I'm looking at some unusual people.

A lady will take a guy's shoes and clothes and dress just like her man. Take her hair up, put it under a hat, paint a mustache on, has the man's shoes on, and she'll look better than he ever did.

A guy will take his wife's dress and things, wigs and jewelry, and put the lipstick on, slip into the brassiere and it looked like a lady. The only thing that was a problem was that he didn't have the lady's shoes on because he couldn't find shoes as big as his feet. So that's the only thing that told he ain't no lady.

I'm seeing the people in costumes, and the Indian's done got drunk and his feathers is falling off, and I'm trying to get home before it starts to get dark outside on a Mardi Gras day.

I was a big hit when I went back to school. That was it for me. That was the end of me shining shoes and trimming rose bushes and cleaning swimming pools. To go to the movies cost twelve cents. From then on it was a different story with that girl. I decided I would be a musician. It was a godsend day for me and it opened up a whole new era in my life.

There was always a set of drums set up in our house. I knew how it worked but I really didn't pay much attention to these drums. I'd play them when Sydney was making his pharmacy runs. That's when I started practicing the drums in our house.

I rehearsed a lot with the radio. They used to play the Top Ten hits every hour, hour after hour, especially if that singer was coming through town.

Shelled Streets

The grain elevator is blowing wheat and grain and chips. You can tell the guys coming from the river work at the grain elevator because they have aluminum shovels. Aluminum shovels are very light. Regular shovels are heavy. I can tell they're loading chips at the river because they have shovels made out of aluminum.

They're all white. Black guys, their complexion from the dust from the wheat, the chaff and the grain, they'd be all white. Their faces and their hands and their clothes—it was all dust and almost phosphorescent. It was like a riddle. What starts life as black guys with white bones and ends life as white guys with black bones? It was working at the grain elevators that transformed some of them, ghost men walking up the road.

They don't wear a facemask. They don't have anything for their eyes. Nobody at this time knows this is dangerous. This is the atmosphere. This is why guys might get an asthma attack.

You have two problems. Some are alcoholic. They drink. I done told you about the drinkers. Others work on the riverfront at the grain elevator. I would watch them through the window walking six or seven blocks from the river and on past our house.

The wheat being processed at the grain elevators is the source of grain for the French families making pastries. Import and export: the wheat coming in and the cotton going out. The town is booming. New Orleans is becoming ever more cosmopolitan. As I practiced on my brother's drums I would watch through the front window as they pressed shells into the street. This shell and tar mixture became the original asphalt.

They come in and lay a hot layer of black tar all up and down this road. Then they come back up the street in with a flatbed truck full of seashells. The truck operator pulls a big lever, the back of the truck raises up, and the guy pours seashells off the bed of the truck. Last thing, this big iron roller machine runs over the street while the tar is still hot—it looks like a giant rolling pin—and it mashes the tiny white seashells, crushing them into asphalt.

This is the original blacktop in New Orleans. That's what the street surface originally is made of in New Orleans. The streets are paved now but they used to be shelled. It kind of mystified me, as a kid looking out that window at 1220 Lyon Street, the visible heat rising off the asphalt surface and how it would wrinkle the air.

Monkey Bars

In the playground right across from my house they had some swings. And they had this contraption: two iron bars on both sides with steps to walk up on, then across the top of it is a metal ladder. At the zoo, we'd see the monkeys swing from this contraption so we called it the Monkey Bars.

The object of it is, you go to the first one, then you swing to the—not the next one, but the third one—and grab that one. And you try to swing to every other one. I was swinging like that and missed one bar and ended up with my arm behind my back. I broke my left arm and they put a cast on it.

When they took the cast off my arm, now my hands were slightly off. I needed to find something to develop my left hand. I couldn't make them balance. So I got these metal drumsticks at Werlein's on Magazine Street.

That's when I started the thing of one lighter, one heavier with my drumsticks. The right stick is heavier than the left one. It came from the metal practice sticks I had to develop my hands and make them balance.

The next thing you know my hands was black. These practice sticks are aluminum so the metal comes off in your hands. So I wrapped white tape around these sticks. I came to like that concept. That's why my wooden drumsticks are wrapped like a tennis player wraps his racquet. I started with that when I was eleven years old and I still play like that today.

Up to that period I was playing left-handed—the left hand on the left ride cymbal instead of playing the right hand on the right ride cymbal. When my arm was broken I could just play with one stick so I learned to play everything with just the one drumstick in the right hand.

Now I'm playing correct. I'm a right-handed drummer now. But I was a left. And it got me to use the right side more. That's what's easier. I became as either handed as a crab. So to me it was a blessing.

Ms. Nermy Calls the Cops

Ms. Nermy liked to drink her beer. It would get to a certain time of the day and she wanted to mellow on out. Beer in her hand, Ms. Nermy used to come and knock on the door of our apartment house:

"Boy, shut up that goddamn noise. Please. Trying to drink my beer. And banging all day? Shut up that goddamn noise! Tell your daddy when he come home."

My dad used to work in Mississippi. So he'd go away for the weekdays and come back on the weekends. So I'd only be with my mother. And these drums all day? And the radio's turned up real loud? So once they called the police.

"In this house there's a band in there. And them guys in there are smoking that weed."

So Ms. Nermy thought—somebody thought—this would stop me from playing the drums. So the police came, and they went to the front door and knocked and my mother answers the door.

"We want to come in and see the band."

"The band—what band?"

The officer says, "I can hear 'em in the next room."

"Oh—okay. I'll let you see the band."

And the policemen open the door. It was me. It was this kid playing the drums with the radio up real loud.

"That's the band?" they said.

And my mother said, "Yes, that's the band."

And I turned around and I thought, *oh shit*. So I stopped playing.

But the police told my mother, "Listen, Ms. Morris. Next time we get a call at the police station saying about the band playing—and this smoking marijuana and stuff—we'll just take the call. But we'll never come back here again."

Now I had a carte blanche to play the drums.

Basket Full of Crabs

A lot of guys' families didn't like the drums in the house. It was too much noise. All my brothers played the drums. My mother would let us play so they would all come to my house to practice. Every day from noon to five we had all these drummers in my house. John Boudreaux and Smokey Johnson was two of the drummers used to practice in my house.

John Boudreaux would play with a guy named Eddie Bo from New Orleans. And then he would play with Huey Smith and the Clowns. Huey Smith was a piano player that was an arranger and writer. He had these four guys singing. And they had a number of hits.

Smokey Johnson used to play with Fats Domino. Fats Domino had five saxophone players.

John Boudreaux is playing like Max Roach and Smokey Johnson is playing like Art Blakey and the guys would say:

"Okay Leo, you take the sticks. Now you play it."

And I'd say, I couldn't play that. But *they were swingin'*. John's playing like Max Roach; Smokey's playing like Art Blakey. And I'm playing like the two of them.

I wasn't a jazz musician. I started up playing what they were playing but I ended up playing something different. It was my brothers who first realized that nobody could play what I played.

Have you ever seen a basket full of crabs?

New Orleans was like a basket full of crabs and I became the crab with the longest legs. The crab with the longest legs starts to crawling over the top—to get out of the basket—and the other crabs is following him and they grab onto his legs to hold on to it; so either he couldn't get out, or he'll take another crab out with him.

This is New Orleans. All you want to do is to do better in life. New Orleans is like a bunch of crabs in a basket. One don't want the other one to get out. Because once he gets out, he's gone. Zap!

Smokey Johnson, John Boudreaux and me, we were all Scorpios. They were more advanced than me because they are about five years older than me. These are the guys I learned how to play the drums from. They did what they were doing but nobody could do what I was doing. We were like a bunch of crabs in a basket.

Valence Street: Cats with Knives

I'm walking down Lyons Street, across Bordeaux Street and on over to Valence Street to the Neville's house with my snare drum under my hand. I can see parked all up and down the block all the cats in the band have 1949 Fords. Black and with the big whitewall tires and parked all in a row, it was a great car for the money.

Fats Domino would get a new Cadillac every year. Paint it sky blue, crème and baby pink. The same three colors, every model year. You'd see that car coming and you'd know it was Fats.

Arthur Neville's grandmother owns all these houses on this block. It might look like a Monopoly board with all the houses she owns. Arthur's parents' house has a big porch up front. When Arthur Neville's band would be practicing we'd sit on their front porch and listen.

We'd walk to the dances on weekends at the YMCA because we could get in for free and we'd stand up by the front of the stage. Sometimes, the last tune, because we were youngsters, Arthur would let Aaron come up and sing and then he'd let me come up and play the drums.

Valence Street is where we learned all our music. Then I walked back home toward Coliseum Street come dark.

John Cook lives on Coliseum. He is known to me as the boyfriend of one of my sister's best friends. He is a bad cat who plays the drums. And as I'm walking home I can see the cats as they would come out of the bars fighting.

There is a nightclub, two bars and a restaurant in this neighborhood. In the restaurant they gamble so anything can go down. Dice. Cards. They gamble Nine Ball on the pool table. I like to stand at the window and watch. Pool balls rifling across the smooth green felt and smashing into the side pockets. I like to watch the geometry and the percussion of it.

Too young to go inside the bars—and I never did like the taste of alcohol—I would just be standing outside the bars seeing who's going inside, who's fighting, who's drunk. Sometimes they might start shooting at each other. It was a lot of activity on Saturday night.

Pow, pow, pow, pow.

When my mama hears the commotion of the guns she would gather us up, Aaron Neville and me, whatever kids is out there. Any mother on the block will do this; they'll take you inside their home.

"Come inside now. Come inside this house, boys."

Cats would be hiding behind the buildings behind my house. Might be cut, might be shot.

Sunday Morning, six o'clock mass and it's dark outside. I'd come out of the house and be going to church with my mother. It was peaceful in the morning. But by afternoon it was all so-and-so got cut last night. You would see the blood trails from the bar and leading all the way to the cat's house that got cut. John "Scarface" Williams got cut this way. A lot of cats got cut like this.

John Cook the drummer is even more notorious for cutting guys with his knife than on the bandstand. He carries a stiletto for which he has a special pocket sewn inside his trousers where he hides the knife. He can instantly produce a knife from his clothing.

The stiletto is thin—a little bit wider and about as long as a pencil. When he takes the blade out it's twice again the size of the handle. He would sharpen that blade and rub raw garlic down on it. When John Cook cuts a cat the wound would stay open. That means he marked you. The skin could never come back together again. As much as you sewed it, the skin would stay apart. He cut a couple of guys like that; there are a few cats got scars on their face.

So I was in it, man. I was *in* it. Seeing cats fighting. I was inside of all that.

Section Two

Trouble

Trouble

I had seen in the movies how you can cut the putty off the window panes and the glass would drop right out. We knew where the mother kept the key but it wasn't under the flowerpot that time. So I took my knife and cut the putty off. That was the fingerprint on the door knob. I came up with the idea.

We stole a Winchester rifle—just like in the television show, "The Rifleman." We stole a .45 automatic pistol. We stole a .22 carbine army rifle. And we stole a BB gun. We hid the guns inside another friend's house that lived around from the school. That's where we got our guns for the gang.

But somehow or another one of the guys takes the stuff away from where we hid it and brings it into Green Junior High. It's in his locker and it's after school time.

The girls are finishing with Physical Ed class at the gymnasium and they have these shorts on. And he sees this girl who he liked a lot and he asked her to have an affair with him. She must have told him to step off because he gets mad, goes back to the school locker, and he grabs the BB gun. He returns to the gym and he shoots her in the leg with the BB gun.

She goes to the principal and says Lloyd Martin shot me in the leg with a BB gun. The principal looks at her leg and he thinks: A BB gun? There were some guns stolen recently and one of them was a BB gun. And he says:

"Let me go down and look in Lloyd's locker."

He goes and he looks and all the stolen guns are back in Lloyd's locker.

Next morning on the public address system in the school it says, "Leo Morris and Lloyd Martin come to the principal's office in five minutes."

So when I get to school—which is well after school time starts—they said go to the principal's office. I was in trouble.

"What?" I was nervous because the police is there.

"Sit down," they told me, "You were in this robbery."

"Okay. You got me."

We had broken into one of our friend's house whose dad was a gun collector. Then Lloyd comes to school—he's late two classes—and they sent him straight to the principal's office. He comes up and he sees me sitting down. He sees the principal, the police is there, then he sees the police report. And then he sees the ink tray on the principal's desk. In those days they used fountain pens and they had the ink tray on the desk.

Before they could ask him any questions, Lloyd grabs the ink tray and throws it on the principal and in one fell swoop like a falcon Lloyd jumps through an open window.

There's a balcony outside, which is about fifteen feet above the ground. So Lloyd flies off that balcony—that's where he bailed from—and he splits.

Trouble—The Aftermath

Next morning's local newspaper reads: "Leo Morris and Lloyd Martin Arrested for Stolen Guns."

I spent one night in the juvenile's home downtown. It's a Boys' Home because they don't have a jail for boys. They make me call my mother on the telephone. My mother's mad as a hornet. She has to come and get my ass. My brothers want to fight me. My dad's away in Mississippi, working. I'm busted. They got me.

When my dad comes home my mother tells him what happened. He looks at the newspaper and rolls it into a pipe. He doesn't whoop me with it, though, but he says something to me.

"I wish you would have shot somebody or killed somebody instead of being a thief. I've never had a thief in my family. You're the first thief."

Then he says, "If somebody says to you, 'Am I your dad?' say no. Because if they ask me if you are my son, I'm going to say no!"

Then he didn't speak to me no more. I couldn't go outside. My mother kept me inside. So it wore on me like that. My uncle Leo, who had been to jail and so he knew the jail thing, he explained it to my mother.

"Listen. Let him go outside. Because you're keeping him in, his anger is building up. So when he gets outside he'll be wild. He already did wrong. He's not doing wrong no more. He already did wrong. So give him a chance to do something right."

It just so happened that my dad would go to the bar room and he would hear this shit about his son and he would be real hurt. My intention was to make this up to my dad. I kept doing good, kept doing good, kept doing good.

Thirteenth Birthday Present: 12-Inch Reels

My mother bought me a GE tape recorder with the twelve-inch reels for my thirteenth birthday. I listened back at that machine to develop my sound. I would check out my left hand, my right hand and my bass drum. That's how I knew what I was going to develop.

"Why aren't you playing the bass drum?"

"I'm too short," I told my mama. "My feet can't touch the pedals."

"Well, get up off the seat."

And so I stood up and started playing like that.

"Okay. That's what I want to hear. Play that one. Now play that one."

That's why I play the bottom a lot—it's because of that tape recorder. I would play back what I had done and I could hear this sound. I could *hear* it. I could hear the bass drum coming back at me. *I could hear it.* Do you understand what I'm saying?

So I developed the right foot on the bass drum. That's why my foot is so strong. It's because of that tape recorder. Those things were great for that—those twelve-inch reels—they were great. I recorded a lot of stuff on that.

My Rhythms

All my rhythms are based on two elements. It's so simple and that's what blows people's minds. The two elements are the Second Line bass drum patterns, and the tambourine rhythms from the Indians dancing at Mardi Gras. Those are the two elements.

My bass drum patterns are from the bass drum player marching in the Second Line. I play from the bottom up. A lot of drummers play from the top down so they very rarely understand what's happening down there. You always hear my bass drum because I'm playing from the bottom up. Don't try to play more that what's supposed to be played because the Second Line is just so simple, man.

The second part of my rhythms is the tambourine patterns that the Indians play while they're dancing to Mardi Gras. I capture those rhythms between the hi-hat cymbals and the snare drum. The Indians, they play these tambourines and they play these rhythms, man. It's unbelievable, the rhythms that the Indians play.

I go back to the house and I try and play some of this on the snare drum and the hi-hat cymbals, mirroring the tambourine. I'm trying to duplicate the bell sound of the tambourine from the Mardi Gras Indians. They can make the bell ring a lot or just a little. I work at getting a similar sound with the tip of the stick playing the hi-hat open or closed.

Steam Pressure Machines

Ms. Nermy has three steam pressure machines—three of them—and when things are slow we go over there and press our clothes. These steam pressure machines, in order to make it lock down, you put the clothes in and you step on this big handle.

You mash your foot down on it and it would say: *Cracka-chew*. And then to release that machine, to make it open up, you press down on the side lever and as it releases it says: *Pssst-taugh*.

To the pressure the machine jumps open. It releases this envelop of steamed air and you can smell the cleanness of the steam and the corn starch. That's the opening and closing of the hi-hats. The sound on my hi-hat cymbals comes from these machines.

These pressers are big iron slabs. So they have three machines going with three different people pressing clothes. I'm practicing the drums next door and it drives them crazy.

I hear this: *Cracka-chew . . . pssst-taugh. Cracka-chew . . . pssst-taugh* over and over again. And I begin to capture the sound of the air pressure by mimicking the sound of these steam machines as they lock down and release.

I found myself trying to duplicate the sound of those steam pressure machines on the hi-hat cymbals. I'm hearing rhythm in these machines. This becomes part of the rhythm for our neighborhood. Practicing the drums next to Buddy's Cleaners, I started copying this rhythm: *Cracka-chew . . . pssst-taugh*.

"What is this you're doing? Where did you get it from?" Arthur asked me.

"I listened at the steam machines," I told him.

I developed this concept at Buddy's Cleaners and Pressing Shop because we pressed all of our clothes there. Cats were sharp in our neighborhood. We played sharp and we dressed sharp.

First Set of Drums

Arthur Neville would walk through the neighborhood and put the band together. One day he came looking for me. There's a knock on the door. As I go to open it, I can see through the window Arthur and his daddy are standing there.

"Look man," Arthur says, "John Boudreaux left the band and we need a drummer."

"We know you don't have no drums," Mr. Neville says.

"So if your brother can loan you the drums for this weekend," Arthur says, "then you could play this gig with us."

My older brother Sydney was a clever guy. He had begun delivering prescriptions on his bicycle for the neighborhood pharmacy. And the chemist who was making the prescriptions was a drummer. But the chemist's wife told him if he hit one more beat on the drums, she was leaving him.

So my brother says to me, "You like the drums, right?"

"Yes, of course."

He says, "You want to buy them?"

I went out for the weekend with Arthur Neville and we did four gigs in three days: three nights and one matinee. We came back to New Orleans on a Monday and I had a hundred and twenty dollars in my pocket. So I gave my brother a hundred and fifteen dollars. Now I had my first set of drums.

My mother taught me how at the end of the night you had to loosen calfskins—both top and bottom heads. Traveling down south the weather is hot. You couldn't leave them tight at night because when the heat came up the next day and the air got dry the skins would pop.

My first set of drums was the Ludwig drums that I had been practicing on in the house. Bass drum, rack tom and the wood snare drum—that was it—painted blue with a gray stripe around the middle. I added a floor tom but the color didn't match.

I didn't care how they looked. Having any kind of drums, you wanted to preserve them and learn how to play them because drums were extremely hard to get.

I told you that I would be practicing when John Boudreaux and Smokey Johnson might come by the house. I was fifteen years old and doing the rehearsals with Arthur but the rehearsals was at Arthur's house. There was a period when this little kid who was like five or six years old would come by because he could hear the drums and he liked the drums, and he would come up directly to the screen door at the Neville's house.

Zigaboo Modeliste wasn't actually playing the drums yet. He was in the neighborhood but he wasn't playing the drums at this time. He would come listen at us rehearsing at Arthur Neville's house and he would be so interested in what we were doing that he would have the screen door impressed into his forehead when he walked away.

So Zigaboo was taking an early interest in but not yet playing the drums at this time. It's interesting because it represents a striation comprised of three New Orleans dummers, John Boudreaux, myself and Zigaboo, convened at the same place and at the same time.

A near-elder to me, John Boudreaux has a very unique style. He sits up straight and he always plays the left stick tradition-style with his wrist. When I joined the Hawkettes I brought another perspective to the drums. I'm playing the backbeat on the snare drum where I want to play it—not playing the backbeat on the two and four all the time. And I have more of an unorthodox style of playing the bass drum.

The lope of the bass drum player who plays in the marching band—the Second Line beat—that's my rhythm on the bass drum. That's one of the things what I brought to the band. And I'm syncopating with the left hand and playing something else with the right hand. You get people dancing. Your feet starts to move. The people on the dance floor got to do something.

There is a private club for white members only on a little side street past St. Charles Avenue and right down the block from the Neville's house. The Valencia Club isn't for black people. We began playing there a lot. The band is making $18 per gig for each band member and Arthur is probably making more than that as the leader. We began playing there quite a bit to get started. The Valencia Club is where the band got tight and we begin to roll.

Gunsmoke and The Ninth Ward

Arthur Neville's dad is a cab driver and he has a Ford station wagon. This is our transport. Five pieces and all the instruments in Mr. Neville's taxi. Only problem is, when Mr. Neville comes home at night from his shift he wants to watch the "Gunsmoke" television program.

We can't walk in front of the television set until a commercial comes on because he likes the show "Gunsmoke" so much. When the show would end, Mr. Neville would drive us to the gigs. We had to schedule our transportation around "Gunsmoke."

The band is Arthur Neville on vocals and piano, Alfred August on guitar, August Fleuri, who we call "Sticks," on trumpet, the saxophone player is George Davis and myself on drums.

Meanwhile, my brother Sydney purchased a practically new set of Slingerland drums for himself. Grey mother-of-pearl finish with a piccolo snare drum. The money I gave him, he takes that money and buys the Slingerland drums from the chemist who he had been working for making deliveries.

But I don't give a damn. I've got my own set of drums. I start my career from that point and with those drums. Now I have a set of drums, man. And I am gone. I'm seeing areas of New Orleans I have never seen before.

The town of New Orleans is cut up into sections. The sections are based on the roadmap of how they originally divided up the city. They call these sections Wards. My girlfriend Ruth Cooper is living in the 9th Ward.

The 9th Ward is interesting because it was originally all swamp land. Backed by the industrial canal, the waste from the city is sent there to be processed. The government sold that land to a lot of black people fleeing out of the city and who landed there because the land was very cheap. They would drop off cement and the guys would build their homes real fast from the ground up.

People got the opportunity to own their own house. A lot of poor black people moved back there and it became one of the roughest areas in the City. Many bad cats lived there.

One time I had a gig with Arthur Neville at a club called the Sanchez Center in the lower 9th Ward. Keep in mind that Mardi Gras is a day of fun and enjoyment, but it's also a day when people used to have some kind of confrontation with somebody. Pickpockets, pimps, all these bad cats be getting even with guys that did something during the previous year.

Gets to where the crowd is having a good time, cat gets stabbed with a knife, gets beat up—then the perpetrator, whose wearing a costume, splits into the alley. Throws his costume in the trash can, puts on another one and goes back out. See, this is New Orleans. This is New Orleans, man.

High Noon

The dance starts at noontime, which is the height of Mardi Gras. The place is packed—I mean packed where you can see purple smoke up on the ceiling—that's how many people were there and smoking weed and drinking.

I knew it was going to be a hot day so I set the drums up right by a window where I thought maybe I could get some cool air. And when we play the first tune, a fight breaks out, and the next thing you know everybody's heading for the window. The floor was instantly cleared.

It's just two guys in the middle of the floor. It looks like maybe they have some knives and the next thing you know we heard some gunshots. *Bam, bam, bam!* Women screaming, folks stumbling over one another to hit the exit, the people had starting stampeding and they're heading my way.

The people started running right at me because now the window is the main exit. And as the people start going out the window they're taking parts of my drum set with them. I had to go out the window and over a fence to chase down the bass drum and some cymbals.

But it was interesting because we only had to play one tune and the dance was over. They had to close the place down. We got the instruments, got paid and went home. So that was my first professional High Noon on Mardi Gras Day in New Orleans. And you better hope no John Cook shows up at your gig.

Mardi Gras Mambo

The Hawkettes record "Mardi Gras Mambo" in 1954 and it becomes the Mardi Gras theme song. We're playing that at a dance and I do this real hip, hard drum beat and it gets everybody up and dancing. We get everybody out there dancing and the crowd says, "Stop the band and let the drummer play."

The next thing I know the whole rooms is swaying in the same motion in sync with the drum beat. When I stop everybody starts screaming. That knocks me out. I didn't know the drums could do that. I didn't know the drums can be that powerful.

The Hawkettes are working every weekend for the top disc jockey in New Orleans named Larry McKinley of WMRY. Every weekend he has another group coming in; another singer. So I'm working every week.

The band is playing with the artists who have the ten top tunes. Whoever is hot from number ten up to number one, that's who we back-up. The benefit to me is that lots of different style artists are coming to New Orleans in the mid-fifties.

Big Joe Turner. LaVerne Baker. Muddy Waters. We are playing behind all of them and they love us. There are a lot of successful resident artists, too. That's how we end up with Larry Williams.

My mother had been sending my dad to work on Fridays with a ham sandwich.

"What is this ham sandwich every day? You been holding back on my money?" We use to afford it only on Fridays. "What are you doing?" he asked her.

"No," my mother tells him. "Your son is doing that for you."

Ham for Pop

I'm scared. I'm nervous. I don't know what's going down. My dad isn't speaking to me.

My sister says, "Pop wants to see you."

He never wanted to see me. He never said anything to me. For over a year my dad didn't speak to me, still didn't say nothing, because he was still upset.

I had embarrassed the whole family. He was upset with me because I was a thief. I had gotten in trouble with a gang in New Orleans. No one had ever been in trouble before so I was seen as the black sheep in the family. It is Sunday night and my mom had just served a nice dinner. All of my brothers and sisters are there. And now it's just my father and me.

"How are you doing?"

"Okay," I said.

"Did you make this record?" He pulls away a cloth napkin that covers a desert plate, only the plate doesn't hold a desert—it's a 45 record I did with Arthur Neville.

"Yes. I made that record."

Everybody in my house was crying. My daddy's eyes are wet, and everybody crying.

"Are you working?"

"Yes. I'm working with Arthur Neville now."

He apologizes to me and I make up to him. Emotionally, it has a very heavy effect upon me. Once I made up with my dad—and my dad made up with me—I buy enough ham for my dad for a whole week. That was a luxury for him.

You've seen those big hams in the grocery window? In those days ham would be cut fresh in the grocery store. The butcher would say how many slices do you want, and he would take his biggest knife. Slice, slice, slice. Just keeps slicing.

This is the evening that set the wheels in motion. It's amazing—just that situation alone—how much it changed my life. How much I prospered.

How much money I made. There was no limit to what I could do. I was making so much money making these records and sending my dad to work every day with ham sandwiches. Now he was my dad again.

From this moment forward my dad and I became tight. And the family is tight. You have to make things happen for yourself in this life. My family is religious people. Yeah, they fight with each other, but they love each other.

Like two cats that don't know each other after they get full of whisky. But past that, man, my daddy is the sharpest thing. He was clean. He was sharp. Knows how to match clothes.

I bought him a canary yellow sweater jacket. Next time I saw my dad he had some black pants on and a pretty shirt and a panama hat.

"Oh," my mama says, "why did you give him that jacket?"

"Mom, it's because I want him to have it."

"Black as he is, he got a canary yellow jacket?"

But it looks great on him. Because he knows how to match it. My dad is dark. My mother is French. She's light. So between the two of them, we're looking like we're looking. And I shot out of that like a rocket.

1957: Larry Williams and the Hawkettes on the Road

My mother didn't want me to go. I was too young. But I was with the band with Arthur Neville and that was the band Larry Williams wanted. The Hawkettes went on the road with Larry Williams in 1957.

It was at dusk when Larry came around the house in a brand new station wagon that he had bought for the band. The wagon was painted white and on the side was painted "Larry Williams and the Hawkettes band" in gold. Underneath was freshly painted "Short Fat Fanny" or "Bony Maronie"—whatever was the hit songs that he had at that time.

You did your own advertisement. You had the radio for promotion. But then you'd put your name on your car or your station wagon. Come through town, folks would look to see whose station wagon it was. It drew attention.

My mother didn't care how much attention you drew. My brother Weedy had been out on the road before me and so my mother knew what goes down with music and musicians. Weedy went through the whole thing: smoking the weed, drinking—and she didn't want me to be a part of that. But I was in the band, had our name on the side of the touring wagon, and Larry is coming around the house because I was holding up the band.

Helen and Larry Williams convinced my mother everything would be fine. I would ride in their new Cadillac with them. Larry promised my mother that he and his wife Helen would personally take care of me and protect me from that. He was about twice my age. I was seventeen. But to my mama I was still the baby in the family.

As soon as we get to Mobile, Alabama, Larry pulls the Cadillac off the road and up into the backwoods in search of Preacher Brown's house. Eventually, we locate Preacher Brown's house hid up behind a row of pecan trees. After a while Larry comes out; he's got a brown paper bag full of reefer.

A number five bag of reefer is a foot and a half tall and a foot wide—and it's packed full of marijuana.

He says, "You know how to roll?"

I said yeah. I roll up some and we're smoking. That is our first stop of the tour, Preacher Brown's house, in Mobile, Alabama, this is our first gig. Larry finds the keys and points the Cadillac north.

On the Road: Part Two

By the time we get through Georgia and South Carolina, North Carolina and into Virginia the guys in the band are dragging. The first three weeks on the road we're moving every night. Night after night we're moving. We're working every night.

We had to drive some place to get a room to sleep and there was nothing for us but guesthouses. And the guys are tied. They're whipped. The guys are drinking this white lightening and can't get enough sleep. But every night I'm playing great. I seem to be the only one in the band that's got energy.

Because it's a guesthouse, meaning there are two, three guys in one room, bathroom down the hallway, I can hear the guys talking at night:

"This cat have asthma?"

"And every night he's playing the drums like a crazy man."

"He must be taking some pills for that asthma."

"And maybe them pills got something in them?"

And one night the trumpet player caught me smoking a reefer behind a tree.

"Oh, okay," he says. "That's how it is. That's how you get the energy. Give me some! I'm going to call your mama—tell her you're out here on the road smoking this shit."

Next thing you know, another guy in the band busts the trumpet player smoking reefer. So the trumpet player ends up giving some to the bass player to keep him quiet. It's a domino effect. And, as this is happening, Larry's bag is going down and down and down.

So Larry says, "Man, what you smoking up all my shit?"

Because meanwhile the guys are saying, I'm calling your mama tonight. I'm calling her. Tell her you're out here smoking that shit. And he didn't realize I'm giving it to the band.

We made it the whole summer of '57 like that up to Washington, D.C. and into Chicago.

Opening up for Eydie Gormé at the Chicago Theater and the band is elevated about four feet off the ground. That's how high the band is. And the theater has so many seats we can't see the faces on the people in the audience. That's how big the theater is. That's how it looks like from where we are, up on the stage.

On The Road: Part Three

Larry Williams is jumping up on the instrument, puts his foot on the piano keys, turns and starts running up and down the aisles. Cats in the band are jumping off that stage onto the ground, running through the audience with them horns. This leaves just me and the guitar player and the bass player on the bandstand. The rest of the band has done jumped off the stage and they're running wild through the audience.

Come the end of the show, Larry and the horns come back up to the bandstand and the audience is going wild! We end the show with our closing number and we're ringing wet from just the three of us playing. Get backstage and I would ask the guys:

"Say, what do you all do when you get out there in the audience?"

The saxophone player is George Davis. He says, "I run back there to the last seat and sit down and watch you all." He's laughing.

Then I asked the trumpet player, who we called Sticks, the same question. Sticks says, "I be looking for the ladies."

And I say, "You mean you've been *talking* to people?"

And he laughs. "Yeah, man. What did you think?"

I couldn't see the people. So I say, "I thought you all were *playing*, man."

Larry says, "Man, you were great today. Thank you very much. Man, you're a great drummer."

And he hands me ten dollars.

"Yeah, but all of my shirts are wet."

We're ringing wet from just the three of us playing. So then Larry hands me another ten dollars—maybe gives me twenty dollars.

It was a great time because I was a youngster and I was traveling. I was seeing cities like Washington, D.C. and Chicago for the first time. It meant a lot to me because before I went out with Larry Williams I had never been outside of New Orleans.

By the time we made it to Washington, D.C. I had made up my mind that I didn't want to live in New Orleans any more. But by the time we made it into Chicago I had a change of heart. I did a flip-flop in my thinking. I had had enough of the cold weather. And when we got back home, where I had had an affair with a girl and she became pregnant, I made up my mind to move back to New Orleans.

French Ancestral Influence

I was married at eighteen. My mother made me get married because she was trying to save me from what might occur without me marrying this girl. My mother didn't want me to have this stigma standing on me. My mother was trying to teach her children the right way to go. So I was married at eighteen.

"We are human beings first, and then we are who we are after," she said. "And the people you are with are human beings."

Growing up we had this French ancestral thing happening. My mother was French and she spoke some French around the house. When she was angry she would say:

"*Mauvais compagnons vous apportent de la mal chance.*"

She was saying if you be with bad guys, you're going to do bad things. Don't be with them boys hanging on the corner. If you're even just standing there they'll take you too. It was because of my uncle Leo, he was the reason why. He was the example in our family. Plus, there was my older brother, Weedy. She had seen his life, the twists and turns.

Weedy was a companion of Earl Palmer. Weedy played so great that people were scared of him. He was one of the first two black cats in the United States Navy Band. The other was Solomon Spencer. Weedy was the snare player and Mr. Spencer was the bass drum player. The same Mr. Spencer was my music instructor in grammar school, junior high and high school.

When Weedy came home he would take guys' jobs and they hated him for this. He was so great that it got to where he couldn't work no more. The people were that scared of his playing.

So be careful who you are with, she'd say. Be careful what you do. If you do something and you have to apologize then check yourself so you don't do that again. Because it's easy to say I'm sorry. Just saying I'm sorry doesn't rectify the thing that you did. Be careful. If you do something and it's not good, then you have to rectify it. You've got to try and make this thing right.

My mother said that whenever I got down and felt bad I should go to a church and light some candles. It's kind of a primordial thing because each fire is all fires. The first fire and last fires lit are one and the same. I used to go into these churches and light these candles and the next thing, my connection with the Lord became close. I developed a sensibility about people and how to raise a family.

My mother made me get married to this girl to show me morals. I couldn't just have this baby with this lady in New Orleans. My mother wanted me back home. But the people didn't mind if you didn't get married so long as you took care of the kid. It's so free here.

If a lady likes you she'll approach you. And she'll be your girlfriend. And you can move into the house with her mother, her father, sisters and brothers. This is your room. This is your house. But you're not married to her. Then you have a couple of kids and the dad says this is my son-in-law. This is how it is in the home, living in their house, without being married.

Now, don't do anything with any other woman because the dad will kick your ass and the brothers will whip you. *And she will kill you.* This is New Orleans, man. It's free. It's so free here.

But my mother persuaded me I had to get married. And doing that made me have more morals about what a man is supposed to do. And that meant in part earning a living and supporting a family. I painted windows. I was working for my uncle Henry. It was my brother Sydney, me and Uncle Henry. We were one truck and a three-man crew. I wasn't paid but $40 a week. I was a window painter specialist. I specialized in windows.

Don't Play the Backbeat

One Sunday afternoon a guy asked me to do a jazz concert with him. His name was Clarence Ford. He was one of Fats Domino's saxophone players—he had five saxophone players—but I had never played jazz.

"I want you to do this jazz concert."

"I don't know jazz."

"You could do it," Clarence said.

A couple of weeks before this rehearsal, my brother-in-law took me to a jazz concert at the Y. Normally at the Y, they'd have dances and everybody would be dancing. That's where we used to go to dances.

This time, they had all these folding chairs on the floor. How are we going to dance with all these chairs? Everybody's sitting in chairs and they're snapping their fingers. I didn't understand what was happening. I was trying to figure out, when are you going to start dancing? My brother-in-law says to just stop talking and listen.

Ed Blackwell had his band. Earl Palmer had his band. These were the guys who were in New Orleans. These were the jazz guys. So that particular setting made me know who was Earl Palmer, who was Ed Blackwell.

On the stage there were two sets of drums already set in place. On the left side, Earl Palmer had a brand new Ludwig sparkling silver set of drums. Earl Palmer was making a lot of records with Little Richard. And he was doing a lot of dates with Fats Domino. Cosimo's Studio in New Orleans was where all the dates were. Earl Palmer was a great session drummer. He was the king of the backbeat.

Earl Palmer had a special speed pedal called the "Ghost" pedal. Professor Solomon Spencer and my oldest brother Weedy had been in the Navy. And there was a guy in the Navy who was a drummer and a machinist. And this guy came back from service making these "Ghost" pedals, based on a patent he developed while working on a Navy aircraft carrier. The name of the carrier was nicknamed "The Ghost." Earl Palmer played the "Ghost" pedal. He might have got it from Weedy or Solomon Spencer. Earl and Weedy were best friends.

Over at the right side of the stage, Ed Blackwell's kit looked like someone had made it by hand. It had a snare drum without the snares for a tom-tom and both the floor tom-tom and bass were 16 inch drums.

Earl played and it was great. Then Blackwell's band played, and I had never heard anything like that! I would see Blackwell and ask him questions. Blackwell was a cold-blooded jazz player. He and I became very good friends. Eddie became my sweetheart, man. But those bands didn't play a lot because there wasn't so much straight-ahead jazz around.

So we were rehearsing at Ellis Marsalis' house one Sunday afternoon. I could get through some of the songs. But when it came time to playing fours, I couldn't feel it. I'm trying to understand what's happening with this jazz music. I had no idea what the conception was. Just somehow or another, Blackwell came to see Ellis about something.

"Hey Blackwell, how do I play this jazz music? Show me how to do fours. I can't do these fours. I'm trying to count it, but I can't come out right."

"You can do it, man. But why you tryin' to count it?"

"Well, Black," I say, "show me how to come out right then."

"Okay," he says. "Let me sit down."

And he sits down to the drums and plays a couple choruses. I can hear this concept.

"Okay, now you take the sticks."

I sit down and I play it. I get through it—a few bumps and bruises—but now I understand this concept. I can hear it. And I can feel it.

"You can do this," he says. "Just don't play the backbeat."

"But what do I do with the left hand?"

"Do something else with the left hand," he says. "You can do whatever you like with the left hand. I don't care what you do with it. Just don't play the backbeat."

And he keeps repeating, "Just don't play the backbeat."

Now that was my first experience of playing a jazz concert. I didn't like it. I didn't like jazz because the jazz guys didn't work a lot. The jazz guys would work once a month—like this and that, here and there, in bits and drabs. I didn't gravitate toward it because there was no money. My family had a lot of kids and relatives and I had to find a way of making money without asking my mother.

I see the jazz guys and they have on the same suit they had last month. So I'm thinking no, I don't want to do *that*. I'm married. I have a kid to support. I have to find a way of making money. This is the period when I move my family into an apartment house on Law Street, in the Creole section of New Orleans.

The Music Business

When I was first married we lived on Law Street in the Orleans Parish. But soon after, because we ran into some hard financial times, my wife Grace, our daughter Shawanda and I moved from Law Street into my mother-in-law's house on New Orleans Street.

The next week there's a knock on the front door. Joe Jones is standing there. I recognize Joe because he lives right across the street from us. The Larry Williams period is well over. Arthur Neville's band is cold. The jazz cats aren't working. I'm doing gigs here and there and doing trim work painting houses. This is when I met Joe Jones.

"They say you're a good drummer," Joe Jones says to me. "If you're as good as they say you are I'd like you to join my band."

Joe Jones is one guy in New Orleans that knows a lot about the orchestration of music. Joe's the guy who put everybody into the business part of music. Harold Battiste, Melvin Lastie, George Davis, Alan Toussaint—different guys would learn how to copyright music from Joe Jones.

Joe asks me to play a gig that afternoon with his band. So I go that afternoon and play the gig with the Joe Jones Band. Melvin Lastie is playing cornet on the gig. And the guys are checking me and looking at each other and they reached the conclusion that I am as good as they heard I was.

So after the gig, Melvin Lastie pulls me aside. Melvin tells me that because I play so great I can join *his* band too. Melvin is on the gig with Joe but he's recruiting me on the side to play in his band too. But I had already committed myself to Joe.

I began spending more time across the street at Joe Jones' house than my own house.

New Orleans is so thick with rhythms because of the many mixtures of people that the French put in the original colony. The French, the Spanish, the Africans, the West Indians—all different varieties of people. Black people, Jewish people, people who sing the blues, people who sing gospel.

Joe Jones' band is playing for the burlesque houses with striptease girls. We're playing Bar Mitzvahs. We're swinging Dixieland. If the kids at a Tulane fraternity have been to a football game in Hawaii, they want to hear those sounds when they come home. Everybody wearing hula skirts, leis around their necks, they want to hear music with the hula. The guitar player puts the tremolo on and we've got Hawaiian sounds going.

We had to play something that represented Calypso and the Caribbean. You have so many varieties of people you had to know how to play their music. Successful musicians, the guys who are working a lot, know how to play all types of music for all types of people. It makes a nice gumbo.

I would be sitting on the floor in the afternoon sunlight, surrounded by Joe's papers, documents, sheet music, him showing me how to copyright songs, how to send five dollars to Washington, D.C. to have his music copyrighted.

"Copyrighting, that's where your money comes in," Joe's telling me. "You write a song. It becomes a big hit. Money starts coming in. You get a check from BMI every six months—for life. They have to pay you for this. Every time somebody records your song, you get paid. And it keeps getting paid. It doesn't stop."

He teaches me how to talk to the agents. Joe explains to me how to get more money from the club owners. But I never paid attention to him at that time. It doesn't click with me. I let it go in one ear and out the other. I don't like it because I think it's like politics. I don't take it to heart.

If the people are dancing then that's it as far as I knew at the time. I'm busy trying to take care of a family at a young age. I need money. I don't need no paper. You could keep the paper. I need money.

I had been on the road. I've been making hit records. I know that part of it. But I don't know how to read music. I want to know how to read the notes. And the guys in the Joe Jones band say I should take a drum lesson.

Drum Lesson from Paul Barbarin

Paul Barbarin was the premier of drummers in New Orleans—of the seniors, at that time—who was experienced to teach. He was Louis Armstrong's drummer. There were a lot of great drummers in town, but only Mr. Barbarin knew all of the methods of teaching how to play the drums.

"Mr. Barbarin, I want to take drum lessons from you."

"Okay, where do you live?" Mr. Barbarin said, "I'll come to your house."

He would come to your house because you had the drums set up. If you were going to take a lesson at his house then you might not want to leave. The best way to get him to agree to give you a lesson was to have him over to your house. That way, as soon as he was finished with you he could leave.

He took the streetcar the next week to my apartment house on Law Street across from Joe Jones, downtown in the 7th Ward, where I lived when I got married. Mr. Barbarin settled into a folding chair I had just set up next to the drums.

From the beginning of the drum lesson—how to place the sticks in your hands—when he saw my method of holding the sticks he didn't correct that. Having seen my brothers hold them, I knew the traditional grip of the drumstick. Mr. Barbarin recognized this was correct.

"Play the introduction to Bourbon Street Parade," he said.

I played it perfect. I had learned it and played it in the parade when I was about nine years old.

"Play a waltz," he said. And I played the waltz of "Blue Danube." "Play a mambo." And I played a mambo beat. He was rubbing his chin and checking me out. Then he says, "Play a Cha-cha." And he turns to me and he says, "Son, I'm a busy man. I don't have time to waste."

"Mr. Barbarin," I said, "I want to learn how to fast-read notes." That means you can read the top line, then you read the line under, and before you get to the bottom line you've already memorized that so you turn the next page.

"You go to school?"

"Yes sir." I said, "I go to Corning High"

"Tell Mr. Solomon Spencer at the school to show you how to fast-read notes." Then he says to me, "Listen, one day you're going to be a great drummer. But when they say to you that you're great, let it go in one ear and come out the other."

Mr. Barbarin looks me cold in the eyes. He pinched his thumb and index finger together, then draws his thumb across his throat.

"And give me my two dollars!"

That is the only drum lesson I ever paid for in my life. I had one drum lesson paid for in my lifetime and it was with Mr. Paul Barbarin.

Press Roll

Professor Solomon Spencer called the open roll a "Mama-Daddy." In order to get it to register in my mind, he would have me say, "Mama-Daddy." It would make me think of my mother and father. That's just an open double-stroke roll. The other type of roll is a closed roll, and it's called the press roll.

The press roll means that you're pressing the tips of the drumsticks to the snare drum and rolling it. But it's also a technique more than that. It's a technique that you put the stick on the snare drum and start from the rim or start from the front of the drum. Never start from the center of the drum. You don't want to start there.

I'll start from the front of the drum and come to the center, then open it up back to the side—moving the sticks in and out. There are so many different sounds in a drum, all the way from the rim to the center. That's one aspect of the press roll.

It's also the way you hold the left stick and caress the thumb. The thumb is where you press the stick to the head. And in the right hand—it's the two back fingers and the thumb that control it. When you're pressing down, then you can hear the sound come up.

Another consideration is that the snare drum heads must be tuned properly. The snare drum heads—both top and bottom—must be in the pitch so when you're doing it you can hear it right away. The snares of the drum has to be put in a certain spot so that when I'm playing—and I want to make this press roll—the snares are loose enough to where you can hear it. That's what that is.

I sometimes put the stick in a certain part of the drum and make the sound come *at* me—it's not so much having the sticks going into the drum. It's an old-fashioned marching thing that I learned from the street bands in New Orleans: to press-roll the drum and make the snares vibrate enough. And you can use the arm in a certain way to make it come out.

The snare drum player plays in the marching band, that's what he does, that's all he does, and he's playing a press roll, and he's playing these beats, and occasionally he's hitting on the rim of the drum—that's where he gets his accents from.

So the press roll is more than what they say it is on the surface of it.

Section Three

Roots Of Rock 'n' Roll

You Talk Too Much

Joe Jones comes up with this concept of people talking too much. It's ironic the song is called "You Talk Too Much" because Joe Jones has the gift of gab. Joe knows how to talk his way into any situation and get what he wants out of it. He can talk his way inside any door. Then they might have to *throw* him out. And that's exactly what would happen with Joe sometimes.

We're running down the song and the band is saying, *I think we got something here.* So we go in the studio and we record it. This is the first time that I can remember hearing the top of the bell played with the stick. I come up with this during the solo of the saxophone player.

"You Talk Too Much" goes number one with a bullet. Because of the sales of the record, how fast it's moving up the charts, the bullet means more than big sales: it means it's fresh and it's moving up the charts fast as a bullet.

Everyone is saying that I contributed to this becoming a hit record because this is the first time this concept of playing the bell of the cymbals had been done in drum period, in playing funk music. Everyone is hearing this concept and the drummers start taking it and using it. This new sound and this technique became famous because they all start copying it.

We made a lot of money with that song. It was double great for me because the Joe Jones band is based in New Orleans. I'm not a businessman. I'm this kid who has a talent. And Joe is a big influence—supping me up, telling me how great I am. I don't have no idea.

Joe is slipping me ten, maybe twenty-five dollars more than the other guys in the band for the dates we were doing because I'm so good for his music. Joe is pumping me up. And I'm pumping the band up, making the band happen.

Sam Cooke and the Dooky Chase Diner

I was upset. My wife wants to go to this dance and I'm fussing with her all week because she and her girlfriends are making plans to go to the dance. Sam Cooke was touring New Orleans with a band called The Upsetters.

The Upsetters is the same band that used to back up Little Richard. I didn't want her to go because I knew who they were. I didn't care for The Upsetters band because I knew how they played. They *danced* more than they played. They come in town—you had to lock your wife and your daughter and your sisters up. Because they take *everybody*, man. You won't have no wife when them cats leave town.

Dooky Chase is a famous black-owned restaurant where you could go in and sit down. Some restaurants you can't go in, but you could get take-out around back. Dooky Chase has a sit-down area that serves blacks. It has a take-out window out the backside.

As I draw near the take-out window I can make out the figures inside. Sam Cooke is sitting inside eating his dinner. He's complaining to Joe Jones. Sam doesn't like the drummer with The Upsetters. So just then Joe sees me through the window getting a take-out sandwich and Sam is complaining and Joe's looking at me.

"The drummer? Wait a minute," Joe says. "My drummer is the baddest drummer in town! Wait right here." And he steps outside to talk to me.

"Leo," Joe says to me, "Sam is having trouble with the drummer."

Joe takes my arm and leads me to table where Sam and he are sitting and talking. Seems the Upsetters, some of them anyway, are as checkered as the tablecloth. I set my sandwich down. Things are cooling off with Joe's band. I sit down to the table to find out what they want with me.

"Do you know any of my music?" Sam asks me.

He starts singing. I start beating on the table. The three of us are laughing. He hires me on the spot. Joe's not the kind of guy that would hold you down. In fact, Joe Jones was my catalyst.

Five minutes at the Dooky Chase Diner and now I'm Sam Cooke's personal drummer. Sam is the star so he goes on stage last. That gave me time to go home, eat my sandwich and change clothes. The house is dark, the house is empty. The wife is gone to the show.

That evening my wife is in the audience with her girlfriends. I take the stage with Sam. That blew her mind. Next day, I was gone. I was out of town with Sam Cooke.

On The Bus

Doing a month of one-nighters with Sam Cooke, it's hard to maintain a relationship. We got the boy bands like the Drifters and the Cleftones on the bus with Sam Cooke's band the Upsetters. Then we got the girl bands with us on the same bus: the Orlons, the Crystals, plus Little Lester Phillips and Dionne Warwick and so forth.

All of us together doing 30 one-nighters in a row, the bus is rolling right along. But the scenery inside the bus is stationary. And remember now, there aren't many hotels for blacks in the South—and its 30 one-nighters in a row. There was this singer on the bus named Eloise Laws who a lot of the guys were hitting on. I don't bother nobody. I'm just a chain reefer smoker. I just want to play the gigs and relax.

"That drummer, he's all the time smoking reefer . . ."

". . . and going to get us busted."

I can hear the people talking. But I just mind my own business. I'm sitting next to Little Esther Phillips on the bus one night.

"Look," I turned to Little Esther, "this girl wants to sit next to me."

"These guys are after me," Eloise Laws says to me. "Could I sit next to you?"

"I'll move over there," Esther says, and points at an empty seat. Then she points her finger at me, says, "But if you touch her you'll be in a lot of trouble."

I don't bother nobody. All the time smoking reefer, the people on the bus were only worried that I was going to get us all busted. But I don't drink. And I don't bother nobody. And then I started sitting with Eloise Laws, who was with the Orlons.

One night Eloise Laws and I broke into a conversation. We talked all night, the sun coming up and us still talking. I tried three or four times that night to get loose of her. As time goes on Eloise begins liking me so much she starts buying me reefer. She would buy me weed and she would buy me shirts. But I'm still married to Grace and we've got a kid in New Orleans.

So I came up with a plan to disentangle myself from Eloise.

"You don't own me," I shout at her next night on the bus. Some of the cats in the band heard me. *Good*, I thought, my plan is working. "Get out of my face," I told her.

I thought that would do it. But the girl chases me down like somebody chasing a rabbit! She kept after me, kept after me, kept after me.

See, during this time I already have a nice girlfriend in New York too. She's a dancer with a dancing group called the Parkettes. The Parkettes would be on the shows when we performed in theaters. This was a different circuit. This was a five-week circuit in various theaters. My girlfriend who performs with the Parkettes is named Deborah.

Deborah is so nice to me. Deborah touches my heart. I never had a real woman that touched my heart like Deborah. But I'm only twenty-one. Deborah has a little boy, and I don't know how to accept somebody else's kid. This girl is a woman. She used to rub me down on my shoulders and then jump on top and put me to sleep. I really liked her but I didn't know how to deal with the kid.

She had a guy, but the guy is a junkie. I didn't realize I probably would have learned to take care of someone else's kid. I saw this in New Orleans. And he's calling you daddy—but you ain't his daddy. I was just too young to figure all this out.

"The worst thing I hate in life is a junkie," she told me one time.

Deborah is my girlfriend and I like her because she was a woman. But I know I had to leave Deborah. And before long I have this other little girl chasing me. LaLa Brooks, who was the singer with the Crystals, she starts to chase me around. I'm still married to Grace. Eloise is buying me reefer and shirts. And I still have to come up with a plan to disentangle myself from Deborah. Man, it wasn't easy being on that bus with all these women.

I came to New York with Sam Cooke. I called up Deborah. Then I called another friend and she brought me some heroin. I remembered that Deborah hated junkies. And I shot myself in the arm with heroin. I did it purposely when Deborah took me to her mother's house in Harlem.

She took me to her mother's house in Harlem to see the little boy. The only way I could figure to get away from Deborah was to pretend to be a junkie. I get in the corner of a back room, roll up my sleeve and put that needle into my arm.

Deborah walks in the room. She looks at me. She looks at the needle in my arm. And she turns around and walks out. I never saw her no more. Now I still got girls chasing me on the bus, and a monkey on my back because of the way I left Deborah. The thing weighing heaviest on me is how I left Deborah in New York.

Pinstripes and Chain Gangs

It's not unusual for us to be doing one-nighters that are five-hundred miles apart from where we played the last night. Traveling with Sam Cooke through the south, it got to where a busload of black people on tour can't find a place to eat. At bus stops we can go to the bathroom. But then there are places we can't go to the bathroom. Places, no place for us to stay. So we have to sleep on the bus until the theater opens the next day.

But we have a white bus driver. He tells them who's on the bus. Maybe they'll let us get a take-out because we can't go inside the restaurants and hotels. Every night: sleeping on the bus, eating on the bus; being on the road involves a lot of human trauma. But I always avoided problems.

I never had any confrontations in my career with racial stuff. My family always taught us to respect everybody. I see trouble coming and I go the other way. Being involved with a gang in New Orleans, I got three years' probation and my probation officer, after a while, he just let me do my things because I was turning my life around. Had I kept up with the bad ways I might have gone to prison.

Tailor-cut trousers, custom-made jackets, Edward Knapp shoes, there was a tailor on Rampart Street in New Orleans that custom-made my suits for me. I wasn't going to wear no horizontal pinstripe suit like they wear in jail. I got away from trouble in New Orleans and I never looked back.

When I was on the road with Sam Cooke, that's when Arthur Neville got The Meters together in New Orleans. When I got back home, Arthur and I were shopping for clothes on Rampart Street. And I said to Arthur:

"Was this the guy on the drums that was a kid watching me when we was rehearsing at your house? But that ain't what I was playing."

Because Zigaboo Modeliste has his own style of playing, a real funky way of playing: left hand, left foot, right foot, and right hand—independent. And this created another sound within Arthur's band, The Meters. Zigaboo got some stuff happen that was like no other drummer that I've heard. Nobody plays like Zig.

We became friends when I returned to New Orleans but I didn't really know Zigaboo too well from before when I lived there. He was this kid watching us practice. I knew he was watching, but I didn't have no idea. But that's a link between Arthur's band The Hawkettes and his band The Meters.

When Sam wrote the song, "Chain Gang," we're back on the bus; we're looking out the windows and seeing the prisoners on the chain gangs in North Carolina. Sam is throwing them cigarettes. And an hour later he has the song together.

When we went into the studio and recorded that song I took the drumstick and put it to the base of a microphone, hammering on the microphone base to duplicate that sound we heard. I was continuing to develop how to paint a picture with the rhythms. That's one of my favorite things—how to paint a picture with the instrument.

"Chain Gang," "Wonderful World," "Cupid," these are big hits and we toured all up north as well. But the band had had enough of the cold weather up north, Chicago and so forth, so Sam signs us up in the spring of 1960 for a tour in Jamaica. Flip Wilson is the emcee at the club where we're performing, called "The Cat and the Fiddle." Flip and I met backstage and he and I become very good friends. And we'll rekindle our friendship several years later in New York.

The tour in Jamaica is over and we're headed back home to New Orleans. June Gardner, who's an elderly drummer from me in New Orleans, he calls me up on the phone.

"Hey man," June says, "Sam offered me the gig as his drummer. And I took it. But you could have my job working in town."

We did a cross. June Gardner goes with Sam. I take June's job in New Orleans. But now my wife is mad because I'm not with Sam Cooke. It doesn't matter to me. I'm barely 21 years old, with a wife and kid, and I have a job. So it's cool as far as I know.

I never asked Sam what had happened. What was the reason why? I never try to call Sam and ask what the matter is. I never did that. I just took the steady job in New Orleans, from which I ended up with Joe Jones again. And back out on the road.

Stranded in D.C.

It's 1960 and we have the number one song, "You Talk Too Much." Joe Jones would talk to the promoters on the side as we were playing these different places. When we got to Chicago, Ahmad Jamal had just opened his club called The Alhambra.

Ahmad's club is serving only fruit drinks, and it's packed every night. I walk into The Alhambra to see Vernal Fournier play the drums. I don't know him but Vernal is a friend of my brother Weedy in New Orleans.

Everyone is so happy that Vernal is playing drums with Ahmad. Vernal had just made this record "Poinciana" with Ahmad. There's a street beat that Vernal put on "Poinciana," and guys are arguing about. Philly Joe Jones, Charlie Persip and a few other drummers are arguing about the way this particular song is played—that it is more than one drummer playing this beat.

At the Alhambra that night I can see Vernal is playing with just the left hand on the hi-hat; and then he takes it to the cymbal and he's playing with his right hand between the snare drum with the snares off and the floor tom. He doesn't have a rack tom—just the floor tom.

So I met Ahmad and Vernal the same night.

"One day, we'll play together," Ahmad says to me.

"Sure," I say. "Let's go."

Remember now, I'm not a jazz musician. I am a funk player. I am in the money-making zone. Playing jazz, just playing once or twice a week doesn't suit me. But Ahmad and I get to know one another and we become friends that night.

Meanwhile, Joe is off talking to the promoters and constructing a cross of his own.

"Hey look, man." Joe would say, "You like my band?"

And they would say, "Yeah, the band is smoking."

"That's great." Joe says, "Because you can book me without going through the agency. You don't have to pay that 15% to the agency. You know what I mean?"

The band was working through the Shaw Agency. But Joe would talk to the promoters like that. When we get to Washington, D.C., the band has a few days off.

So this particular day, we had the day off and I decided I'd like to go to the movies. I'm sitting in the movie theater watching the Western—just sitting and watching—when I see this guy coming through the aisle with a flashlight.

"There he is. Right there! That's him!" And they put the light right on me.

When I see this guy coming down the aisle with this flashlight, I think he is trying to show somebody to his seat. In those days, they used to bring you to your seat in the theater. It's dark and they would have a flashlight.

"Come on," he says. "You're coming with us."

"What are you talking about?" I said.

"Come on, guy—get up from there." And he shines the flashlight right on me.

"Hey man. What's the matter?" I said. I'm trying to watch the 'shoot 'em up' movie.

"Shut up," the people said. "We're trying to watch the movie."

"What's wrong with you all?"

"Get out of the theater!"

"Come on, man. Come outside," he says. "I need to talk to you."

It was Maxine Brown—who was on the tour with us—it was her manager. Joe did something and the Shaw Agency is mad. We get outside the theater and I see my drums are strapped on top of this station wagon.

"Why did you put my drums up on that wagon?"

"You're going to New York with us," he says.

"*New York!* I can't go to New York. And where's the rest of the band at?"

"We're taking you with us."

"Wait, wait—no—wait a minute." I say. "Let me go back to the hotel. Let's talk to these cats, find out what's happening with Joe Jones."

Maxine Brown

Back at the hotel, Maxine Brown's manager had already got into my room while I was watching the movie. Cleaned my room out, packed all my clothes and my drums without me knowing it.

How Joe would talk to the promoters got back to the Shaw Agency and they fired the band. They fired the whole band. So we were stranded in Washington, D.C. I think we managed to get through two or three weeks of the six-week tour and now the band is fired. They're going back to New Orleans.

Everybody is sitting around all droopy and sad. The guys said for me to go ahead with Maxine Brown. They were going back home.

Maxine's band wagon pulls to the curb at the Apollo Theater in New York City. I look up at the marquee and see the names Jimmy Reed and Jerry Butler. Maxine Brown is opening the show.

"Leo," she says, "I'm sorry about stealing your drums. I want to buy you a new set. Go down to Manny's Music and pick out a set of drums."

I picked out a set of silver sparkle Slingerlands.

Opening night, Jerry Butler comes out and watches me playing behind Maxine.

"There's that drummer." I can hear him telling the guys, "Man, that drummer's bad." I can see him thinking, *I wonder what he would play for me.*

After the first week at the Apollo Theater, Maxine Brown takes a two-months' vacation. So I made two weeks with Joe Jones and one week with Maxine Brown and now Jerry Butler is hitting on me to play for him.

So I go out with Jerry Butler and never went back with Maxine. All this happened inside of a month between Washington D.C. and the Apollo Theater in New York City. I did a triple-cross of my own, but I wasn't done yet, Dee Clark watching all this from the wings.

1961: Dee Clark and Jerry Butler—Energy vs. Ice

Bobby Scott's band used to back up Jerry Butler and Dee Clark. Both guys were on Vee-Jay records. The guy who was cold would open the show. The guy who was hot would close the show. Whoever could get a hit record first would close the show so everybody on the bill was trying to get a hit record. I'm with Jerry Butler now so Dee Clark is watching me play every night. I'm playing with Jerry and the Bobby Scott Band.

"Oh man, I've got to have this drummer," Dee is telling the guys. "Listen, Jerry. I'm going to use this drummer. And you keep using the original drummer from Bobby Scott's band." That's how Dee got this energy behind him. That's when I started playing for Dee Clark.

Dee Clark would go on before Jerry Butler and we made it so hot that Jerry couldn't get on the bandstand. By the time we finished—poor Bobby Scott's band—it wasn't no place for them to play at all. Because Dee and I had *wiped them out*!

Guys like James Brown and Joe Tex would be running up and down the stage. Joe Tex was very theatrical. He knew how to do things with the microphone that was innovative. And other cats knew how to dance. Jackie Wilson knew how to dance. James Brown knew how to dance.

But Jerry stood in one spot and sang like that. Then he did a little twist and that was it and he walked off stage. They called Jerry "The Ice Man." The difference was that Dee Clark was an energy singer.

Dee liked this band so much that he wanted to record with us. The band went down to Miami and we recorded "Raindrops" in the Spring of 1961. "Raindrops" sold over to million copies. That whole album is great. This is when I met Phil Upchurch and we became good friends.

Phil Upchurch was Dee Clark's favorite guitarist. Phil Upchurch was Dee's musical director. Phil went everywhere with Dee. In truth, I think Phil Upchurch helped Dee write "Raindrops." By the same token, Dee Clark would help Phil write his hit records like, "Can't Sit Down."

And through this whole period of when I was on the road with Dee Clark, Jerry Butler is plotting on how to get me back into his band. *That drummer. That drummer. That drummer. I've got to get that drummer back.* But then Dee left Vee-Jay records and I crossed back again and did go back to work with Jerry Butler.

Traveling with Jerry Butler

The band is Jerry Butler, Curtis Mayfield and Leo Morris. The promoter had these neat little six week promotional packages. The Howard Theater in Detroit, The Royal Theater in Baltimore, the Uptown Theater in Philadelphia, The Regal Theater in Chicago and the Apollo Theater in New York City.

You would have to have a hit record to be on the show at the Apollo Theater. Sometimes they would have eight or nine artists doing five shows per day at the Apollo. Some of the artists only did their hit record or maybe they did two songs.

This is when I met Little Stevie Wonder. He could play anything. We were on the show and he wanted to play the drums. When I got to the drums, he had popped a head on the upper tom-tom. I didn't play the way you would break a head.

Because of the mileage we were putting on the car, Jerry Butler would buy a new Cadillac every model year. End of the year came, Jerry would buy a new car because we had worn the old one out. At the dealership Jerry would have them install four General "Dual 90" tires on the car before it left the lot.

These special tires wouldn't blow out and you couldn't puncture them. They cost $115 extra. He had to spend that much because we couldn't carry no spare tire because of the stuff that we were carrying in the trunk. It was just the three of us and our personal driver named Jai Johnny Johnson.

"Jaimoe" was the driver, but he wanted to be on stage so much with the musicians that he bought some bongos and he asked me to show him a few beats. I did that. And then he bought a conga drum. Then when we went on the stage he brought the conga and he brought the bongos. Most of the time he was waving his hands more than he was playing the hand drums. He couldn't really play but he just wanted to be up there.

We didn't carry our instruments at this time. Just a suit bag made out of leather, where you could have four suits in there, four pair of trousers, four white shirts and a nice pair of Edward Knapp shoes in the bottom of the suit bag—that was your wardrobe. And then you had another, smaller bag for your personal accessories.

I had my chrome over brass Ludwig snare drum, my drumsticks, and my brushes. There wasn't no other drums or cymbals at first. I played whatever that was provided and I had to make them sound like my drums sounded on the records. After a couple of years I began to carry a single cymbal. Because of traveling without a drum set, this made me develop my thing on the snare drum.

I had the snare drum tuned to the room—might be a club, might be a ballroom, might be a tobacco warehouse in North Carolina. But my system is that I turn just one or maybe two lugs to bring the pitch up or down. Same thing with the bass drum. If the pitch is too low all I had to do was turn two lugs and take it higher. Then during the concert, I would bring it up or bring it down.

I'm going to tell you one of my tuning and performance secrets. When the singer doesn't have the energy and the concert might begin to drag, I will tune the bass drum up a pitch to make the singer or the soloist come alive—to make him pop the vocals stronger and better, to put some energy behind him. That's what we were doing on the road.

When I first played the Apollo they had the big bands. You would put the drums on the platform and they would just roll the drums out with the band. You would be about two feet above the floor. You'd play with the singer, and then they rolled the drums back off the stage.

Chain Reaction

They put the spotlight on Jerry. This is a bright light, man. Because my drums are rolled up right behind the singer this huge white spotlight is aimed directly on me too. I can't see anything out there. And it's very, very hot. As I'm playing this light is bothering me.

One afternoon I come out the back exit of the Apollo Theater and as I'm walking along 125th Street in Harlem I spot an eyeglass shop. I look in the window and I see these black glasses that have yellow lenses in them. I buy those glasses and I wear them on stage that night.

Now it is cool because instead of having the bright light being white, now it was yellow; so that toned it down some. That is the reason I started wearing sunglasses when I perform. It's not that I want to look cool, it's because the lights distract me when I'm playing. Sometimes my eyes are closed.

Look up one night and Sam Cooke is watching me. He sees me before I see him. Ordinarily after we finish the first half of the show, we change clothes, pack up the car and split to the next gig. But this night Jerry and Sam are on the same bill.

Jerry Butler is closing the first half of the show. You'd have about eight or nine acts to go. Then Sam Cooke would close the second half of the show. Sam might come out to the wings of the theater in his bathrobe—where the audience can't see him behind the curtain—and watch me play. He looked like a boxer before he goes in the ring.

We didn't have far to go that night so we stayed to watch Sam's show. Sam is upset because he thinks I quit his gig.

"Hey look." Sam says, "I want to see you."

"Solid," I said. "But what do you want?"

"Come on," he says. "Let's get on into my limousine and let's talk."

I sat in the limousine and I lit up my joint.

"Why did you leave me?"

"What? You fired me, man."

"I never fired you. Why would . . ."

"Well, the man called June Gardner up. Told him you told me you hired June. And June gave me his gig in New Orleans."

"I would have never fired you!"

"Well who fired me then? Because I ain't with you no more."

It was the guitar player. It was Cliff White who done this. Sam never fired me. It was Cliff White that manipulized this.

Cliff didn't like me because Sam hired me. Cliff wanted an older guy on the road with him as a companion—not a younger guy who Sam likes. And oh, Sam is begging me. "Oh, little brother." And he's hugging me and begging me to come back.

Curtis Mayfield, who is the guitarist for Jerry Butler, that night Curtis says to me:

"Look, I'm leaving Jerry. And you're coming with me. We're going to go and form the Impressions again. I'm going to leave Jerry Butler tonight."

I didn't go with Curtis. And I didn't go with Sam Cooke. And Curtis left just like that.

Fred Cash had been an original Impression when Jerry had been with them. And Fred went with Curtis to Chicago. This is when Sam Gooden joined the Impressions. But the Brooks brothers—Arthur and Richard, who were part of the original Impressions—weren't part of the new group that Curtis was putting together. And I stayed behind with Jerry Butler.

After Curtis left in the winter of 1963 we tried a string of guitar players. First was Harry Pope. There were others. Then comes Larry Frazier.

Larry Frazier

Guys are standing around outside the theater. Pimps, pushers and hustlers. They know the musicians get paid on Thursday night. It's Larry Frazier's first week at the Apollo and his first trip to the city of New York. I'm watching this guy who was waiting outside the back door when he approaches Larry.

"Hey look, man," this guy says. "Could you help me find this address? I'll give you this money,"—and he shows him this money inside a brown paper bag—"if you can help me find it."

Larry looks in the bag. "Sure, man. I'll help you find it. And you're going to give me that money?"

They start walking along 125th Street. The thirteen hundred block; the fourteen hundred block; they're looking up and Larry's checking the addresses at these brownstones.

"How do I know you'll find the address? Maybe you'll take my money and not find the address."

Larry says, "Hey man, I ain't gonna do that."

So the guy says, "Look, you got any money? Put your money in the bag, man. Put your money in the bag with my money, and you can hold the bag."

So he did that. And now Larry is holding the bag with both their monies. They find the address and the guys says, "Thank you very much," shakes his hand and goes through the building and out the back exit.

Meanwhile, Larry's not looking inside the bag.

He starts back to the theater and opens up the sack. Scrap paper. Shit! The guy done switched the bags. And Larry got a bag full of scrap paper! That was Larry Frazier's initiation to the Apollo Theater in New York City.

Larry Frazier is a very good player. He loves jazz. He plays the guitar backwards because he is left-handed. Larry Frazier stands with the band for a while; then he leaves. So Jerry Butler would just hire another guitar player and give him only the guitar parts.

We couldn't get another musical director because nobody could learn this music fast enough. Come a day, nobody is left but me. Automatically I became Jerry Butler's musical director.

Drummer and Director

How can a drummer be a musical director? I've been watching directing. I know how to do this.

I'm not a drummer that plays a rhythm for the song, and plays the same rhythm straight through. I will play the music: the melody, the rhythm, the dynamics and the chord changes—all of this—just like the song goes.

One unique thing about my playing was how I would play with the vocalist and help him sing the song better. Behind the soloist or behind the guy singing the song, I would play the chord changes and play the rhythm at the same time. So this was unique. But I had no idea that I was doing this.

There was something else we did that was unique in the rock 'n roll era. We began rolling the drums out to the very front of the stage. This was unusual that the drummer is at the front of the stage, but that's just what we did. My drums were set up in front of the band, directly behind the singer.

So I'd stand up and turn around backwards, and then I'd say to the band the name of whatever song we were playing next.

I'd say, "one . . . two . . . three . . ." and sit down, play the fourth beat.

And the guys were saying, "Oh man, this is too much." But I was just doing what I saw the musical directors do. And I would cut them off with my back to them because I was the bandleader.

My favorite song was "Moon River" from 1962. That was a big hit. Being on the road, "Moon River" kind of reminded me of the Mississippi River in New Orleans. It didn't take me home, though. That song didn't really take me home.

The guys liked me because I was the young kid that directed Jerry Butler's music. There was never a drummer being a musical director before so it kind of knocked them out. This is a period when I'm recording at Specialty Records for other leaders as well. I did some things for Gene Chandler and Major Lance and so forth. They put me on there because it sounds so good and it sells so good. Things were going smooth again.

During some of those early gigs with Jerry, though, it was chaos and mayhem. Panic and pandemonium. It never bothered Curtis Mayfield.

"What are we going to do? Jerry's mad and he's not going on."

The gig never goes like it's supposed to go. There's always a monkey wrench in it. If you don't have yourself together you'll get cut up.

"I guess everything's going to be alright," Curtis would say.

"But Curtis, they're throwing us out of the theater!"

"Ain't no need in hollering. Everything's going to be alright."

We would end the show with the song, "Your Precious Love." I'd get to the cut off and I'd signal to the band with one hand and hit the rim shot with the other. And then I'd hit the final chord. The lights come down and the curtains would be closed.

Thunder

I used to watch Elvin Jones play with John Coltrane. God, there was just so much energy. It was a club called Slugs. Slugs had three chandeliers—three chandeliers on the ceiling from the front door to the stage. And when Elvin came in they used to call him "Thunder." They called him "Thunder" because he would play with so much energy he would make the chandeliers shake.

I wasn't playing jazz. I was playing rock 'n' roll with Jerry Butler. But I got to talking with Elvin and he said to me that it was Trane that was motivating him to play like that. He was trying to play what Trane was playing.

Trane would have the horn in his hand all night long. He never would set it down. I can remember another show at the Village Vanguard. After the set, Trane would retreat into the kitchen where he would stuff a towel all down in that horn and he would practice; he never stopped playing; and when it was time for the next set he used to come out like that from the kitchen—still playing—and he would be joined by McCoy Tyner and then Jimmy Garrison and then Thunder would come in. And when Trane would get to the stage, it was on, man.

After seeing Elvin I realized I had to develop my body for endurance. I knew it was partially a physical thing. I was trying out new things that came to my mind. I tried to play the way Elvin was playing behind Coltrane at this time. Elvin has this loping stuff happening. I picked up on that when I used to watch Elvin playing with John Coltrane.

The Portable Record Player

I'm playing rock 'n' roll music and I need to hear something that is different from what I am playing every night. I had met Elvin Jones and McCoy Tyner and Jimmy Garrison and I was so intrigued by their music that I carried their records around with me.

It was four records I carried with me. It was "Impressions" by John Coltrane; "Waltz for Debby" by the Bill Evans Trio; "Sketches of Spain" by Miles Davis. And I had "This Is Our Music" by Ornette Coleman with me because I was trying to hear Ornette's melodies.

Eddie Blackwell was the drummer on "This is Our Music," and he played the melodies right along with Ornette. I was trying to hear that concept at that time. I was listening to how close Blackwell played with Ornette. So I used to listen at that record to inspire me that I could hear something different than what I was playing.

I'm traveling with a beige colored RCA record player that the top, when you take the turntable loose, the top part is the speaker. Get back to the hotel room and I unscrew the white light bulb and replace it with a red bulb. I place a damp towel up against the bottom of the door. I unhook the speaker from the turntable and put the speaker up against the wall, put these records on the turntable.

And I light a joint to relax and hear some jazz music.

Curtis Mayfield: Keep on Pushing

About nine months after he had left the band, Curtis came back to me with an offer I couldn't refuse. The Impressions is the hottest band around at that time. And Curtis Mayfield was the most unique guy I ever met. We'd hit the stage and start an uproar.

The Impressions was Curtis on the guitar, a bass player named Lenny Brown, Sam Gooden and Fred Cash were two singers, and Leo Morris on the drums. So we had a complete group in five pieces that had three singers.

That's when Curtis began writing all these songs. Curtis recorded all the songs in Chicago for Specialty Records. "Gypsy Woman," "Keep On Pushing," "Amen," "People Get Ready." It was unstoppable. The Impressions recorded the nine albums over a period of five years: "The Impressions," "Keep On Pushing," "The Never Ending Impressions," "One By One," "Big Sixteen," "People Get Ready," "Ridin' High," "The Fabulous Impressions," and "We're a Winner."

Curtis had the red Jaguar, Sam and Fred had two red Stingray Corvettes. I always rode with Curtis in the Jaguar. Lenny rode with Fred in the Stingray. And Sam drove the car by himself, everywhere, because I don't think he wanted anybody else driving his car.

We left Chicago to tour down south. We were five black cats that had a red Jaguar XKE and two red Corvettes. By the time we got past Philadelphia it looked like every cop that saw us stopped us. We'd see that black and white Ford with the red cherry light flashing in the rearview mirror.

The cops would pull our ass over. Those cops would pull *our ass over*, man. One cop shines that flashlight on us, while the other one leans up against the window, the two of them talking at us:

"Okay boys. Let's see the papers for these cars."

"You own these cars?"

"Where you all going? Oh, let me see . . ."

"You all are musicians?"

"Play *me* a tune."

"That'll be a hundred dollars."

See, we were used to people paying *us* to play. Shit, that went on all the way down south, man. So we paid the money on the fender. Just put that money on the fender of the policemen's squad car. And every time we'd hit another state, they'd pull our ass over. Same routine all the way down south.

Three red sports cars? Black cats? Stop this shit, man. Because we was smoking; we was flyin' that shit, man. And it was hard to stop.

Driving Lessons

In those days on the road we used to get paid every night from the promoters. And a lot of times they had a percentage, meaning over a certain amount of money that night, the Impressions got a percentage of that money. These would be one-nighters so some of the promoters used to play with you. They would play with those figures, with how many people used to come in the door.

I saw how Curtis handled that. The word got out to all the promoters that this cat is so slick he's got somebody at the door counting people, or counting the money, because Curtis was collecting the money himself. So that's the way he handled it. He was so peaceful. And you can't trick him.

After about a thousand miles of riding with Curtis, one night we finished this gig somewhere in Georgia. And we came out into the night and onto this big parking lot.

Curtis said, "Get in the driver's seat."

"I don't know how to drive this car," I told him. "It's a stick shift and the only thing I can drive is automatic."

"You're going to learn tonight," he said.

We went into the parking lot and we just drove around in circles because I didn't know how to shift the gears. We drove around, lurching and stalling, until I got to learn how to shift the gears.

Curtis says, "That's alright. If we've got to get a new transmission, that's alright. But you're gonna learn how to drive this car tonight."

I eventually learned how to shift the gears. Curtis taught me how you could double-clutch to synchronize the gears and the motor when you downshift. The only problem I had was when I had to stop and pay a toll on the Pennsylvania Turnpike. Pitch some coins into the basket, the light turns green and the gate swings up and I'd get panicked. I'd pay the toll, but then I had to get it into first gear. I pulled the shift lever in the floor into first and dropped the clutch. We couldn't get out the toll booth, man. Once I got out though I was cool.

So we traveled through the south with that fleet of red two-seater sports cars. Every three-, four hundred miles the cop pulled us over.

"You know you were clocked ninety miles an hour!"

Five black cats touring through the south? A lot of attention was attracted. A lot of attention. Too much attention. But I always liked to drive that car for the power of the Jaguar. That was a great experience, running the XKE through the gears. We were on the road, man.

When we finally got back to Philadelphia we said let's find somebody to drive these cars to Chicago for us. We never took that fleet out again. Curtis kept his Jaguar, but the two red Corvettes we let go. So we never did that again. We got a station wagon instead.

People Get Ready

Curtis had just bought a hollow box Gibson guitar, blonde, gold frets. I had just bought a new pair of shoes. Curtis and I are sharing this hotel suite in Philadelphia. And he's sitting on the side of his bed and he's making up the words to these songs:

"People get ready—there's a train a-comin'. Don't need no ticket, just get on board."

So I said, "That sounds like *something*, Curtis."

He finds the chords he wants to play on his guitar. I take the shoebox, put it up on the bed—take out my brushes. I'm playing on this shoebox with Curtis and we're playing this song, man. Curtis was always working like that.

We got to Chicago and we went in the studio: *"People get ready—there's a train a-comin',"* and I played it the same way I played it on the shoe box. I played it the same way on the snare drum with the brushes. Big, big hit.

We'd get to the studio and he would be playing on the guitar while we listened to the playback. This used to happen quite a bit with Curtis. "Keep On Pushing" was done on the spot in the studio in 1964. The "Keep On Pushing" record had five Top 40 hits on just that one album.

"What is that, Curtis?" I asked him. And he'd say to just be still and he finds the chords he wanted.

"But it ain't in four-four—it's in three."

I kind of put a backbeat to it. Sometimes I'll put a backbeat to a song, but it's not where the backbeat typically is. I put the backbeat where I want to put it. That's one of the things I'm known for, that's maybe one of the things where Eddie Blackwell in New Orleans influenced me. At the same time, I liked the way Elvin played "My Favorite Things" with John Coltrane.

So when we started to running this song down, "Keep On Pushing," I'm trying to play like Elvin Jones playing in three, 'cause it's in three, it's in threes.

Goodbye to Curtis and the Chicago Hawk

Being with Curtis shot me to a whole other thing. During this time we all lived in Chicago. The Sutherland Hotel at 27th and Drexel Boulevard had the Sutherland Lounge inside. That's where all the jazz guys used to come and play. That's where I lived. Lake Michigan was about three blocks north and Chicago is very cold in the wintertime.

You could feel the Hawk when it came out from the lake. The cold breeze that comes off Lake Michigan that makes you feel like you don't have no clothes on—and you do have clothes on—that's what the Hawk is. You could feel it, I'll tell you that much.

We used to flip coins for who's going outside to get the rib tips. The rib tips across the street were thirty-five cents a plate. But neither of us wanted to go. Somebody had to go. Whoever lost the toss had to put on his coat and the other guy's coat too. You needed two coats.

I put on my coat, my friend's coat, two pair of pants, long drawers, and still felt like I didn't have no clothes on. That's what the Hawk is. Winter was coming on when I decided, no—not this year. I didn't want to spend the winter in Chicago so I told Curtis I was leaving the band.

When I said I wanted to come to New York, Curtis was concerned with who I was going to work with and how I was going to make a living.

"What are you going to do?" Curtis said.

"I don't know," I said. "I'll just try and find something. Maybe I'll play some jazz."

And he said, "Jazz? Oh god! There's no money in jazz music."

I checked out of the Sutherland two years after I checked in. When I got ready to leave the guys gave me my pay. Sam Gooden gave me some money. Fred Cash gave me some money. They had a nice leather suit bag made for me with my initials on it. Curtis gave me an attaché case.

He said, "Open it when you get on the plane." And we said goodbye.

I get on the plane, I'm coming into New York, I put the attaché case under my seat and I fall asleep. Then I wake up and I remember the attaché case and that they said open it up when you get on the plane.

I opened it up. It's full of money. It's full of money. It was full of money. I had over $7,000.

So the guy sitting next to me, he says, "What did you do, rob a bank?"

Then I began reading the letter that Curtis wrote me.

Curtis had given me one and a half percent of the publishing. Curtis had several publishing companies. C-Windy, then Curtom—which I didn't even know—I didn't have no idea that he was doing that. But while we were in the band and we were making the songs, he had given me one and a half percent of the publishing that covered these songs.

I didn't even know what the publishing was. I knew what the royalties was from Joe Jones in New Orleans, but I didn't know about publishing. Curtis showed me a check of $65,000 from one of the hit records we did, and I thought, *oh yeah—I should write songs.*

So I had this money. That was the money that I came to New York with. I wanted to come to New York because this lady was here. I left Curtis and went in pursuit of my second wife in New York.

Section Four

Early Days in NYC

LaLa Brooks

I set down my bags in the lobby of the America Hotel in Manhattan. Flip Wilson is waiting for me at the door. We had met several years earlier in 1960 when I toured the Caribbean with Sam Cooke. When we got to Kingston, Jamaica, Flip Wilson was the emcee and a comedian at "The Cat and the Fiddle Club."

New York is fantastic. And the lifestyle of New Yorkers is much friendlier than it is today. People are kind to each other. You can take the subway and get anywhere with no problems. Guys stand up on the train to let a lady sit down instead.

I would ride the F train from the 50th Street Station in midtown Manhattan to Marion Street in Brooklyn to visit future wife number two, LaLa Brooks. There are wicker seats on the subway trains. It's something soft and you can ride on it comfortably—it isn't anything like the orange plastic seats they have today. Ride the subway for an hour and the impression of a wicker basket is pressed into your clothes. All in my trousers and the backside of my shirt—especially in the summertime—I'd have that wicker impression creased into my shirt and pants.

LaLa is her stage name but her birth certificate name is Dolores. She's with Phil Spector's group, the Crystals, the lead singer on "Da Do Ron Ron," "He's Sure the Boy I Love" and so forth. The Crystals is a very popular group.

I used to see her when I was on tour with Jerry Butler. But we knew of each other even before that when she was touring with Sam Cooke. Sam always took the Crystals with him on tour because he liked them so much. But she was just a fifteen-year-old kid when we met and I was married so I promised myself I wouldn't get involved. She was just a kid that used to try and flirt with me. But when I moved to New York City I decided to pay her a visit.

Afternoons I'd take the F train into Brooklyn and then that evening I'd ride the same train back into the Manhattan. Step off the platform at 50th Street and head up the stairs onto the sidewalk. Buy a hot dog—maybe three of them—for fifteens cents apiece. Man, them hot dogs was humming. They were so good that when you bite on one it pops in your mouth. Put some mustard on 'em, drink a Coca-Cola, that's it, man. You're full and it cost only a dollar.

There's an automat called Horn & Hardart on Broadway at East 14th Street. You put a quarter in the machine and you can get a pastrami, liverwurst or bologna sandwich. The automat holds a glass case machine and you put the money in and pulled out the sandwiches. All the cats go there and get a sandwich and a matzo ball soup. And all up and down Broadway they have the hot dog stands. Man, they have them lined up all up and down the road.

Then I might just be walking around. I was cool with it. Many times, as I was walking down Broadway between the union and the drugstore, Jeff Barry would see me and say, "Leo, what are you doing right now?" If I wasn't busy he'd ask me to come to the studio in the Brill Building.

Basket Weave of Light

Jeff Barry is a famous New Yorker who used to write songs for a lot of popular groups: The Crystals, the Ronettes, the Shirelles, the Drifters. Then later it was many other groups like the Monkees—oh man, I used to make a lot of demo recordings with Jeff Barry.

We'd walk to the studio together. He gets on the piano and starts playing these songs. I'm playing the drums. Just the two of us. No other musicians would be there. And we would do just one take. Do about six of them—man, that's $150. Put that in the bank box.

A demo is a demonstration of what the song sounds like. He would put his lyrics with the drums and piano and get this to an artist or a group he might have in mind for this particular song. The artists sings it in their key. Then you get it to an arranger. The arranger will write it out in the singer's key. The staff musician of that respective record's company will listen at it and get as close to this sound as they can. They would have to try and copy it. That's how a lot of records were made.

The light and the shadows interplay off each other in Manhattan because of the skyscrapers. Just walking around, the impression was of being in a basket weave of light.

There is a drugstore at Broadway and 50th Street. And at the back of the drugstore there is a little room with a window looking onto the aisles of the store. Through the window is the owner of the drugstore sitting behind the glass and next to a safe. This drugstore serves as the check-cashing place. The drugstore owner has a safe back there and he has to open the safe and get your money.

Everybody who works on Broadway or is a musician goes there because the union where we get our checks is two blocks north on 52nd Street. I'd go there and cash a whole envelop full of paychecks at a time. For every check, he charged you for it.

Me and the guy got tight because he was making so much money off me. If you were walking around New York you didn't want to carry that much money. So I'd take it to the bank. That's when I got a safe deposit box and began keeping all my money in that.

Hot Plate

Flip is a cold-blooded comedian. We're big time, man. But this apartment at the American Hotel where we were living was small. It is just two rooms and a bath. In order to cook a meal we have an ironing board in the closet that flips down from the wall. I use the closet for a kitchen. I put up some shelves and put my food and canned goods in there. And I put this two-burner hot plate and a rotisserie on the board to cook our meals.

LaLa, when we were courting in the beginning, I asked her to come to the apartment. She was kind of leery. "I could cook you some dinner," I said.

To be sure there wouldn't be no funny stuff go down, she brought her niece with her. And I cooked all that day for her and her niece. I cooked some chicken wings and brown gravy; some rice and spinach. That was the meal I served to them and they liked it.

The niece says, "You got some more? I'll take some more."

So they kind of enjoyed it, my cooking and the hot plate and the closet kitchen too. LaLa told me that on the way home the niece asked her:

"What are you going to do with this here cat? Well, if you don't want him, I'll take him."

Next door is a place called The Alamo that looks like something right out of Mexico. They have sombreros inside on the walls. You can get a big bowl of chili for thirty-five cents. Put some cheese on that and little round crackers. I used to like hot tamales.

There was a guy that had a hot tamale wagon at the intersection of Magazine and Napoleon streets in New Orleans. After the movies we used to go and get some hot tamales. Them Mexicans know what to do with a bean, brother. You'll bite your fingers off eating them tamales. They're spicy like New Orleans.

Then there is a place down in the village called The Bagel. That's when I started eating bagels, toasted and with cream cheese. It is kind of like a Jewish place. We'd sleep right through breakfast because we didn't need it. I had never had a bagel before I moved to New York.

Or we'd go get a pastrami sandwich and root beer—no fries—from Katz Deli. That guy used to send pastrami to the boys in the army. That was Katz's slogan—and they did that.

Flip and I used to make a big pot of meatballs and freeze them. Make some spaghetti, put some meatballs on the hot plate, and put it on the spaghetti. My mama was a cook in an Italian restaurant in New Orleans. She taught me to cook—just watching her—and how people should share. But I discovered there is a difference between New Orleans people and New Yorkers.

Wizard in the Kitchen

One day I went to the supermarket—this was way before I was Muslim—but I knew how to select fresh meat and poultry. And I saw this nice chicken, but it is capon so it's bigger than a regular chicken. I brought him on home and put him on the table and cooked him up. Made some brown gravy—it was out of sight.

The people in the building, all up and down the hallway, would smell this food. I made so much food that people used to knock on the door to know what I'm cooking.

There was a drummer—he was working a lot with Blue Note Records; he was working with Freddie Hubbard. He was working his ass off—and he lived right across the street. One day Joe Chambers came by our apartment house, said he wanted to smoke a joint.

Joe opens the door and the aroma just attacked him.

"Hey man, what you cookin'?"

Joe lies around the house until the food is finished. I give him some, give him a joint and he leaves. So the next day he comes back again.

"Hey man, you got any of that chicken left?"

It was in a big pot so I put it in the refrigerator so I didn't have to cook every day.

Then one day I happened to go by his house. Joe Chambers was living with a bass player named Mickey Bass. And I sat there, we smoked a joint, and their girlfriends were cooking in the kitchen. We would sit and talk, maybe listen to records—and then I see Mickey come out the back of the kitchen and he's wiping his lips. And then Mickey would sit and talk. Next I know, Joe would walk off and then Joe would come back from the kitchen licking his fingers. I'm looking at this and Joe says,

"Oh man, we just had enough for ourselves and the two ladies."

So I found out a lot of cats will just give you the joint, but they won't give you no food. So the guys were saying: New Yorkers, they give you a joint but they won't feed you.

In my house in New Orleans, that's all we do is give food away. We'll force you to have some food. That's how New Orleans is. So that's a contrast between New Orleans and New York. I cook all the time. Neither of my wives could cook. But I'm a wizard in the kitchen.

And living with Flip—and all these comedians, who were his friends that used to come over by the place—I developed a sense of humor. My traces as a young kid and into my teenage years were always serious. I was a very serious type of guy. And it reflected to people like that. So in order to make people a little easier, I try to make some humor. And I learned this type of humor living with Flip Wilson when I moved to New York.

Credit

I began working at a tavern in Hell's Kitchen. From the outside, it is a regular club that serves food and drinks. But on the inside, it is a gangster club run by some very important people. Vivian Reed called me and asked me to join her trio. We worked five nights a week in that tavern. Vivian Reed was the piano player.

Independent and a musician, I couldn't get credit. Vivian Reed told me to go to Bloomingdale's and tell them that I've been here for a year.

"Have them call me," she said. "And I'll say, 'Yes, he's been here a year.' This will cover you so you can establish credit." Due to her, that's when I got my first credit.

Now I have a bank box, but I'm not a big spender. I didn't have no vices. Due to her, I established credit in New York City. This helped me move out of the American Hotel and furnish off my first apartment in New York. I bought a television, a bed set, a sofa—lots of things I bought now that I know what credit is.

They know me at the bank as this guy who comes in with this briefcase and puts his money in the bank. So when I got a little two-room apartment at 2274 Broadway I used my bank account and Vivian Reed as my reference to establish credit to furnish it.

It was a rent-controlled building that a lot of musicians lived in. When one old person moved out, we got the apartment for another musician. We ended up with lots of musicians living in that building. And the rent in this building was very cheap. The rent was $52 a month.

In the apartment above mine lived a percussionist, a Spanish cat named Angel Allende. Tyrone Washington was a saxophone player there. There was James Booker. Woody Shaw, the trumpet player, lived in an adjoining building which was connected to our building. And another trumpet player named Marty Sheller, who was working as an arranger with Mongo Santamaria, lived right next door to me.

Marty liked egg cream sodas. One day Marty said you've got to try an egg cream. We used to come out of the apartment, turn west towards

Broadway, and there was Joe's soda stand. Now, every time I'd leave the building to go to work, I would get an egg cream soda. Might be running late for a date but I always would stop by Joe's first. It was so delicious and it looked like he would put extra stuff in it.

I'd say, "Joe, fix me one. I got to go. I'm in a hurry."

And he'd fix it up—maybe a half pint, maybe a full pint—and he'd pack too much in it. You couldn't close the lid. Egg cream brimming over the rim, Joe would put a piece of tape on it just to hold the top down. I'd be in a hurry so I'd just say to put it on my tab. Then, when I'd come back home I would pay him. So I learned you could use credit in those days.

House Drummer at the Apollo

My days off I would go around and look at the guys playing. It wasn't that I had to do something right away in New York. I was just enjoying myself. I would be all dressed up. I had tailor-made trousers, nice shirt, and slick tie. One day I took the subway up to the Apollo Theater because I used to play there a lot.

I knew a lot of the people so I went backstage and I saw Reuben Phillips, who was the Apollo's bandleader and musical director. Stevie Wonder and the Motown Revue were there. Reuben Phillips asked me what I was doing in town. I told him I had moved to New York and he asked me if I was working. He said, "Man, give me your phone number." So I gave him my phone number.

That week he called me and asked me, did I want the job playing in the Apollo band. I said yes. But the gig was Charlie Persip's job. So he asked me again, did I want the job? He put Charlie Persip on two weeks' notice. And I got the gig working at the Apollo Theater. I stayed there about a year and a half.

In the meantime, I remember Charlie Persip saying that he wanted to come down to the theater and see who is this cat who took his gig. Then he saw me playing and he says,

"Oh shit, I can't play that."

But Charlie Persip and I became very good friends. There was, however, a future incident in Harlem that would strain our friendship.

Natural Blonde Maple Drums

Charlie Persip has this cute little set of drums at the Apollo Theater. I think these are great. When I took his job at the Apollo I have a set just like them custom-order made for me. The grandfather who owns Manny's Music in New York said I couldn't get a sound out of the bass drum because it was too small. But that's the drums I had made. Slingerland natural blonde maple shells. Oh man, everybody loves these drums.

It's an 18 inch bass drum but the shell is only 12 inches deep. It's shallow like the piccolo snare drum my brother Sydney has so I knew how a small drum can be punchier and more powerful than a big one. It has a 12 inch by 8 inch ride tom and a 14 inch by 14 inch floor tom. I already have a snare drum, my chrome over brass Ludwig Supraphonic that started with Jerry Butler and the Impressions.

I love the Ludwig Speed King pedal. It's expensive. And the drop-down catch is a little wide. But the instrument itself depends on how you play the instrument. One thing that works great with this pedal is that the clamp that attaches the pedal onto the bass drum hoop is a little deeper than others so it fits great on the wider bass drum hoops. It fits real nice and snug on the bass drum rim.

Another reason I like it is because it is rounded at center of the footboard. Other footboards of this period are one piece of metal straight across the pedal. But the Speed King pedal is rounded so it's wider than other pedals. Because it is wider than other pedals the benefit is you can move your foot to the right or to the left, and you can still play it well and with a balanced feel to it.

I also like them because in the front of the pedal if you turn the pedal upside down, there are springs there. Take a screwdriver and you can adjust it tighter or you can adjust it looser. You can keep working it. The best way to put it is to adjust it so you can play it well. You have to balance it.

That Speed King pedal is my favorite pedal. That pedal, that pedal, that pedal, man. I made a lot of money with that bass drum pedal! My love of the instrument is that I like the Speed King pedals.

I taped the air holes of the new maple drums up from the inside. Because the drum doesn't have an air hole, when the pressure hits the top head it goes straight down to the bottom head—can't go out the air hole. So I get this sustaining sound. The drums just keep ringing until I stop it. I like that. It's like a piano player putting his foot on the sustain pedal, and the sound will just keep going and going and going.

I experimented on these drums and that's where I got my drum sound from. Because they are so small, I can take my whole set of drums and put it in the back of the cab and go make a gig.

Incident in Harlem: Scorpion

Charlie Persip had a set of Gretsch drums in the pawnshop. They ain't but about $150 drums and he needed $30 to get them out of hock. So he conned me into giving him a lot of money for the drums. He made me think they were good drums. I played them for a little while and then I shipped them home to New Orleans. The heads sounded like you was out pounding on the sidewalk.

And after that I had a run-in with him. I was doing drugs at that time. I was a junkie. I gave him some money and he tried to rip me off again. He starts running and then I tried to catch him as he was going into the park in Harlem off Amsterdam. I ran across the street and the cop car came and almost hit me. I folded on the street. I had on me a nickel bag of reefer and they went in my pocket.

"We got to do all this paperwork for a nickel bag of reefer," the cop says. Meanwhile, Charlie Persip is gone. So I spend the night in jail. The next day they put me in the paddy wagon and they take me to court in Brooklyn. One guy had fifty bags of heroin. I had a nickel bag of reefer.

"Man you got a 33-05," they guys were saying. "The judge going to throw you out of his court."

I wasn't before the judge for a second and sure enough the judge says, "If I catch you in this courtroom again I'm going to get you good. Now get out of my courtroom." And he sets down the gavel.

But that same day I go home and get my pistol. It was time to even up with Charlie Persip. The drums, the drugs, the money—all of it.

Whenever somebody gets you busted in New Orleans we give them a pistol-whip. We kneecap them. We shoot them in the foot. But if they're lucky, we just pistol-whip them. Most of the times I've been tricked it was from people who were close to me. I was a friend with Charlie Persip and I let him get too close to me. I got Charlie Persip in the corner, pistol in my hand. He's pleading with me.

"Oh, man, oh man, please."

And the guy that was with me said, "He knows better than to fuck with you." But every time he sees me he remembers. That friendship was out.

The first time for the robbery in New Orleans I had three years of probation. But that made me a man. My dad said if I would have shot somebody it would have been better. So that put me in position to where I am now. Because I had to prove that I was going to manage that. And I did. But don't bother me.

If you push me, next thing you know your back's up against the wall. I'll strike out at you. They'll say, "Oh man, look, don't mess with him. Don't bother him. He's cool." But if you get me upset—Zap—I'll jump right on you. That's the scorpion in me.

The scorpion is quiet and he goes about his business, but you attack him and he's a sting ya. I didn't know anything about being a scorpion and I don't know anything about the horoscopes. I don't know any that stuff. All I know is that I like peace. I like quiet. I like not to hurt nobody.

Section Five

Introduction to Jazz Scene

.

The Five Spot

I am working at the Apollo Theater and the guys in the band said I should go down to the Five Spot. They say there's a guy down there who plays three horns at one time. So I thought they was drinking too much. I thought they were kind of exaggerating.

The job at the Apollo Theater takes all day, but at night I begin going downtown to see the jazz players. It's something I like to listen to but I can't really play. I can't woodshed jazz because I'm at the theater all day.

I go to the Five Spot and I see it is Roland Kirk. And he *is* playing three horns at one time. And I think, *yeah, that's interesting*. Boy, I'd like to play with him. It was like a magnet drawing me to him. So I asked the drummer, his name was Candy Finch, if I can I sit in.

"Could I play one tune?"

And he says, "Yeah, man. Come on. Sit in."

We start playing. After the melody Roland turns around and says: "Who's that on them drums?"

So I said, "It's Leo Morris."

I ended up playing the whole set. After I played the set this other guy walks up to me.

He says, "I like your playing. I'd like you to do a concert with me in Town Hall."

And I said, "Well I'm working at the Apollo Theater and I don't know if I can get off."

And he says, "Oh man, *please* try. I would like you to play the concert."

And I said, "Okay. Well, what is your name?"

And he says, "Kenny Dorham."

And I thought, okay; but now I'm nervous because I know Kenny Dorham from his playing with Max Roach. That night, it was Kenny Dorham's band, Freddie Hubbard's band, and Lee Morgan's band—trumpet players.

Kenny played first and the guys in the band said, "Who's that drummer? That drummer. Who's that drummer?" They said it was some kid. They didn't know my name. So they said it was some kid from New Orleans.

I met a lot of musicians that night: Paul Chambers, George Coleman, Betty Carter. I've worked with all of them. That was my introduction to New York and the jazz scene. They were all saying I was the baddest cat in town. They could hear the jazz cats were saying:

"You want the baddest drummer in town? Get Leo Morris!"

Checkered Cabs

In New York we travel in Checkered Cabs. Which is a kind of box cab, where the backseat—you can practically walk around inside of it. They have them in England. On the side of the taxis are black and white checks painted all the way around. These are Checkered Cabs.

I like that concept because there was a lot of space between the back seat and the front seat. I could get the whole set of my new drums in the back of that checkered cab. I had the trap case, cymbals, bass drum, and two tom-toms in the back of that cab. It was easy to carry. The bass drum was light. The tom-toms was light. I could take three drums and could go down the steps with the three drums and go back upstairs and get the trap case with the snare drum and cymbals in it.

I see a Checkered Cab. I hold out five dollars. He stops on a dime.

"Look." I say, "There's five dollars for you. I got to go to the Five Spot."

"Okay," he says. And he puts the drums in the backseat. The little blonde maple jazz drums sat right beside me. He didn't put them in the trunk.

In those days five dollars was a lot of money. It only cost about a dollar and something to get uptown so five dollars was a lot of money. But I didn't care. It was so easy to travel with and great to transport. It was just—Bap!

"And step on it!"

Art Blakey's Cymbals

It's blinding white, falling snow illuminated in a beam of light beneath the street lamp just outside the front door. I step through the door and out onto the sidewalk to smoke a joint. A very cold night, man, you can see your breath and the steam coming up out the manhole covers on Third Avenue. I make out two black cats crossing the street and heading right at me. A short one in a tan sheepskin coat and a tall one in a black formal overcoat. This is the night Art Blakey and Elvin Jones come to hear me play at the Five Spot with Betty Carter.

I had been playing earlier that week with Tony Scott, a clarinet player from Italy. And I had just lost my cymbals in the club. It was snowing all week and I didn't want to drag them out and through the snow so I had stashed them inside the club.

Somebody must have seen where I had hid them and they stole my cymbal bag. The first night after, I don't have any cymbals so Tony goes to his house because he lives near-by and he gets his own cymbals. I am playing Tony's cymbals with Betty Carter's band when Art Blakey and Elvin Jones walk in The Five Spot. They hear me playing and between sets Art pulls me aside.

"Son, you're very good. You've got nice hands. But those pot covers you're playing on don't do you no justice. We'll be back when you finished with the last set. I've got something at the house that you could use."

Art and Elvin come back end of the last set and I go out with them into the night. I won't return for three days. It was two days and a half of hanging out before I realized how much time had passed.

"You're one of us," Art is telling me. "And I'll squeeze you until you say that you're one of us."

Art is a very strong guy and he's putting me into a bear hug. So I think, *no. I don't think I want him to do that. So I'll say that I'm one of you all.* These guys are my heroes.

Wednesday morning I get back to my apartment with a set of Turkish K. Zildjian cymbals. The hi-hats are fifteen inches. I had never played hi-hats that big before. So this comes from Art Blakey. It comes from Art's taking an early interest in seeing me become successful. I play them at every gig and in every style of music.

The drummers that I look up to who are in New York at this time are Art and Max and Elvin. These are the guys that I like. Max is a soloist. And Art is the swing. And when I got the okay from these cats—Art and Elvin—then I thought that I could really play the drums. That's why Art gave me those K. Zildjian cymbals. That's what sparked me. They had already proven themselves that they could play. *Well, I guess if these cats say that I can do this shit, then I guess I can*, I decided. So that made me work on my skill. When people heard me play they liked me.

I'm still doing the job uptown at the Apollo Theater, which took all of the day. And at night, I was going downtown to see the jazz players. I am indulging my interest in jazz. But I don't consider myself a jazz player. But a lot of the jazz players were starting to check me out because I have this New Orleans thing going on.

One wintery night I go downtown to see Miles Davis play. A lot of the jazz cats would go to see Mile Davis perform. Lou Donaldson had played with Miles and then he formed his own band. Lou Donaldson wasn't playing that night, he was there just to watch and listen.

Lou Donaldson

I meet Lou Donaldson as I'm walking down the steps of Birdland. Birdland is in the basement of this building, down the street from which is the drugstore where all the musicians and entertainment cats used to cash their checks, at the corner of Broadway and 50th. Lou and his trumpet player Bill Hardman are walking up the steps when they spot me.

"Hey Lou," Bill Hardman says. "There's that drummer I was telling you about!"

Lou has this funny Truman Capote voice. Says three words: "Can you swa-ing?"

And I say, "Yeah-es, man. I can swing."

And he says, "Are you working next week?"

I say I'm not. So he says, "You wanna gig?"

And I say, "Yeah-es, man. I wanna gig."

He says, "Give me your number."

So he takes my number. And the next week we go to Baltimore and we play at Gary Bartz's father's club, The North End Lounge. The first tune we play is "Scrapple from the Apple."

We have Billy Gardner on the organ, Bill Hardman on the trumpet, Lou Donaldson on the saxophone and myself on the drums. After the head, Lou turns to Billy Hardman and says, "We got us a drummer."

The Catch in the Net

I'm a funk player. I'm not a jazz musician. I don't have much correspondence with jazz guys because I'm in another zone. I'm in the funk-drumming zone. I'm in the money-making zone. I make money. I make money. I make money.

I need some money—every week, every night—I need some money every night, man.

Minton's Playhouse. Club Baron. Count Basie. There are a lot of clubs in the city we're playing. Next door to Count Basie there is a place called Wells where we go to listen to some music and eat chicken and waffles. All these particular clubs are uptown.

The stage arrangement at the Club Baron is most unusual. At Club Baron the band is set up and performing behind the bar. The stage is behind the bar. That's one place we are playing. All those people is two feet from the drums and cymbals. And they be talking at me while I'm playing.

"Yeah, play son . . . hit them drums . . ." "Yes!"

"Oh, look at that . . ." "Yes!" "You're bad. Go ahead son. Hit them drums."

And I can hear all this while I'm playing.

"Let the drummer play . . . Let the drummer play."

"Uh-oh . . . look at that . . ." "Look at those long legs on him . . ."

I got thrown into jazz in New York. I got thrown in. They threw me in.

I made one record with Lou Donaldson, "Alligator Boogaloo," and I was tossed into the jazz net. Tossed in there! When they pulled the net up—wasn't nobody in there but me—because nobody could play like me. I was the catch in the net.

Francis Wolff and Alfred Lion are the two owners of Blue Note Records. Frank Wolff is dancing in the studio during the "Alligator Boogaloo" session.

"Keep that beat. Keep that beat. Keep that beat." Frank Wolff has this German accent.

When they hear this beat the guys start dancing around the studio. Their movement is all out of the sync of the music. But they have the beat.

I don't consider myself a jazz player. I'm a funk drummer. People call me a jazz drummer because I make so many jazz records. I remember this happening with the first record date I did with Lou Donaldson at Rudy Van Gelder's in April of 1967. This is my introduction to Blue Note Records. The guys at Blue Note want hits. They want hit records, man.

Rudy Van Gelder's Studio

Rudy has this huge studio. There is this black and white checked bench in the visitors' area outside the engineer's booth. Not in the control booth but inside in the actual studio. I can remember seeing Frank Wolff leaping off this bench at this recording date.

The musicians' studio is rough concrete blocks on the bottom and wood on the top of the walls. The floor is concrete—that real smooth concrete—and then Rudy has carpets by the drums. *And carpet by the guys who stamped their feet too loud.*

The sound of the studio isn't coming from the concrete blocks; the sound is coming from the wood in the ceilings. The ceilings are tremendously high: big wooden beams that make a pyramid at the roof.

Rudy has these baffle panels—each panel is about three-to-four feet tall—which he places one in front of the drums, one on both sides at right angles, none behind or overhead the drums because it is an open studio. This is the original way we record.

Rudy has a double-glass window—about two inches apart—that separates the musicians' studio from his recording console area so the sound won't come through to the engineer's room. There is no other glass in the studio. The engineer's booth is separate.

You couldn't bring a glass of water or a sandwich inside of his studio. That was taboo. There was no way you could do that.

If you make it past the turntables, he likes you. If you get inside the recording console, he really likes you. You couldn't see his board because he doesn't let you but a certain distance into his studio and that was it. Then Rudy has a window to his backyard where there's a series of birdfeeders outside. Rudy has the most modern equipment available. He is the most advanced engineer that I know in the city of New York City. He has the top-of-the-arts equipment.

Cutting a Record

Rudy has a special machine that puts this needle down on a thick disc of an LP. He starts with running the master tape. Then he puts the needle down on it and it cuts right into this perfectly smooth disc. I'm watching him cut records onto the biscuit with these special machines.

One time Rudy has me look right through the microscope. "Do you see anything?"

And I said, "I don't see shit. Why? What you want me to see? What am I looking at?"

I looked again through the microscope that was hooked to the needle. I could see the needle cutting into the record, which it was cutting into the vinyl. Rudy had put the needle down on the blank disc and it cut right into the LP.

Then I looked close to the stylus and the needle had went off the groove. So he had to take that and throw that disc away. He took it off the lathe and he broke it over his knee with a crack! Then he started in with another one.

That's how they make the master—cut right into the groove. That's what makes the sound.

They cut records at Rudy's, but they didn't stamp them there. They never stamped records at Rudy's. They cut the masters there and somewhere else they stamped the records.

This was the original wording of cutting a record. It wasn't playing the music. It was the actual needle cutting into the grooves of the vinyl. This was before acetate. That was cutting a record, man!

Capturing My Sound

When they recorded and when they mastered, they used to put the drums in the back of the mix and they put the horns and the rest of the instruments in the front. But Rudy put the drums in the front and put the rest of the things around me. That's how Rudy captured my sound.

When people heard this music on the radio, the station announcers didn't need to say it was me playing on the drums. They knew it was me. Because at that time, nobody else could play the drums like that. And by Rudy doing this, it helped my career. Guys would hear this drum thing and wanted to know what I would do for them. They loved it.

I was able to play the bass drum on the offbeat, where it grooved and it locked in—but it *swang*. The bass drum beat: it's skippin', it's skippin', it's skippin'. That's one of the things I was known for when I came to New York. That's one of the things I was doing that I didn't know I was doing. That's what all the jazz cats liked.

The "Alligator Boogaloo" date with Mr. Lou Donaldson was very successful. That second line beat will make you move. You've got to do something. Every record that I did with Lou Donaldson was a hit. He had the secrets of making hits after hits after hits.

Rudy made me a lot of money. We became instant friends. And his recording of music was so unusual and so clear that we became instant friends from the first recording that I made with him for Blue Note Records.

Lou's Jazz Lesson

I spent three years with Lou Donaldson. And during this period it seems like there were sections where I would record a lot with organ players. This is one of the things that I was better at than other drummers. So that's why I did all these dates with organ players.

Dr. Lonnie Smith, Shirley Scott, Charles Earland, Rueben Wilson, Emmanuel Riggins, Ronnie Foster, Neal Creque, Leon Spencer, Sonny Phillips, Charles Kynard.

And there was Bill Mason, Ernie Hayes, Don Patton, Richard "Groove" Holmes, Willis Jackson, Wild Bill Davis. These are some of the organ dates I would do. The organ was the thing.

There was only one other cat besides myself that played well with the organ. Donald Bailey, who played with Jimmy Smith, was the other. My older brother Weedy used to play with Wild Bill Davis.

Jimmy Smith and Wild Bill Davis played the organ different from the other guys because they played the bass on the pedals. The other organ guys—in contrast and comparison—only played at the pedals; but for the most part they play the bass with their left hand.

Once the organ player starts playing the bass line on the left hand, and then starts soloing on the right hand, they will begin to incorporate the left hand to playing the solo and they lose the bass line.

As the drummer, you have to keep the time going. You've got to keep it level. And that's what I was good at playing. That's why I made so many records with the organ. It was because my timing was impeccable. And my swing was so hip that you wouldn't believe I came from playing funk music.

This is another lesson in playing jazz music. You sit down to the drums. Don't play the bass drum. Don't play the snare drum. And you'll hear the swing. I had to learn that because I was not a jazz player. But I watched Art Blakey play. He had the strongest hi-hat ever. Why? It's because he was playing the fifteen inch hi-hats cymbals when most guys were playing much smaller cymbals.

The swing happens between the ride cymbal and the hi-hats. Listen to Art Blakey. He will swing you into bad health. Art Blakey will swing your ass into bad health, man. He plays the two and four beats heavy on the hi-hats. Then you've got the pattern on the ride cymbal. So those two match up and that's where the swing occurs.

The other colors are between the snare and bass drums. And you can't be playing up on your toes. You might get a Charlie Horse. So I play heel down on the bass drum and the hi-hat, and rock into heel and toe on the hi-hats. That's what makes the swing happen between the ride cymbal and the hi-hats. I got that from Art Blakey.

Most rock drummers play four-four on the hi-hats. When they start making something on the drums they take their foot off the hi-hats. A lot of them, when they're fixing to make a fill, they take their foot off of the hi-hat—they leave the hi-hat open. But in playing jazz the swing comes from the hi-hat sound.

This concept originates from the guy in Second Line drumming playing the bass drum while he's playing the two and four on the cymbal that's screwed down on top of the bass drum. That's where the swing comes from. And as you press down harder on the hi-hats you can feel the two and four when you play the cymbal beat. Those two are supposed to connect. That makes the swing.

When Art gave me the fifteen-inch cymbals, I had to strengthen the calves in my legs to press down on the cymbals because they were heavier than what I was used to playing. And ever since that time I've been playing fifteen-inch cymbals.

One reason everybody had an organ was because it cut down on the one man, the bass player. We might have four pieces instead of five. It was economical. It was compact. But then again that organ was heavy. It took all four guys just to lift it.

With Lou Donaldson's band, we put that organ on the trailer and pulled that with Lou's station wagon. When we got to the club we had to unload that trailer in the reverse order it was packed. The clothes was the last thing to go in and the first thing to come out. The organ was next, then the Leslie speakers, the drums, Bill Hardman's trumpet (and however many bottles of whiskey he had). Last in, first out; first in, last out. That's how we packed.

It needed all four of us to carry that organ. Each guy would take one handle on the four corners and roll it to the curb. Then we had to lift it up off the curb, roll it to the door and go up the stairs. Take the rollers off and then two strong guys on the back, two guys on the front—we'd pull while the other guys pushed. It just slides right up.

We did the same thing coming down the stairs. Put the legs up and you guide it down. When we got to the bottom, we'd put the set of wheels on it and roll it back to the wagon.

I went to Philadelphia with Lou Donaldson one time. After a weeks' work he gave me a hundred dollars. I had to ask him:

"Where's the rest of the money at?"

"There ain't no rest of the money," Lou says. "That's what the gig pays."

Then I had to pay the hotel out of that. I almost quit on the spot. That was jazz. So after that, most of the time I never went out on the road with the people I recorded with. I just did the records.

The organ was the thing that keyed it off itself. Then the guitar period keyed off that. You can understand why I looked forward to the guitar period.

The Guitar Period

Grant Green used organ players. Every record Grant did for Blue Note records between 1967 and 1971 I did with him. Rudy Van Gelder recorded my favorite Grant Green record, "Alive," at the Cliché Lounge in Newark, New Jersey. So we did play some gigs together. But for the most part we made records.

Grant was a guitarist's guitar player. All guitar players loved Grant because he was so creative. I saw George Benson sit down and watch him play at Club Baron in Harlem. George Benson's jaw would drop—his mouth is hanging wide open—in awe of Grant Green. Grant Green was George Benson's guru.

Grant Green, George Benson, Eric Gale—these were the guitarists I worked with. So this was the start of the guitar period. Grant Green and Eric Gale were two of my favorites. Grant was more creative than Eric.

Eric Gale had a nonchalant attitude about recording music. Now I can see how much sense he made. What he was doing. He would play something that *he* liked but it wasn't on the sheet music. But when we started recording, he only played what was on the paper.

"No!" the producer would say. "Play that what you was playing when you all was jamming! Play that."

And Eric would say, "You better write that down."

"You're the one playing it," they'd say.

"I don't know. I don't know. I don't know, man."

Eric would say for them to write it down. He wasn't volunteering to give any of his music away. And they didn't know how to write it down. But I was the opposite.

The producer would tell me to throw away the sheet music and play something that's hipper than what was written on the paper. And I would do that. I was giving my stuff away. I learned a lot from Eric Gale. Because he was a great leader. I took his advice and considered how to capitalize on it.

The Saxophone Period

There was the saxophone period. Same as the guitar period, the saxophone dates keyed off the organ. Rusty Bryant, Sonny Stitt, Gene Ammons, George Coleman, Houston Person, these are some of the guys who were recording for Blue Note and Prestige Records.

Prestige Records put out titles like: "Black Talk" by Charles Earland; "Black Vibrations" by Sonny Stitt; "The Black Cat" with Gene Ammons. At this period, there was an awareness of blackness. They had black power of the Black Panthers.

There was a pervasive awareness of the two runners who won the gold medal at the Olympics. They put black gloves on and did the black power sign at the summer games in Mexico City. There was a lot of protesting, Martin Luther King Jr., Malcolm X. So it was a black area at that time.

My first album as a leader for Prestige was named "Black Rhythm Revolution." Actually, I never wanted myself to be affiliated with that kind of movement, the Black Muslim movement. But that's where all that blackness came from. Some people were exploiting this blackness.

There was an interesting recording date that I did with a guy named Willis Jackson. He was one of the guys in town who was famous for playing in Atlantic City. We would play in one of those clubs for two or three months at a time. We played into the morning until the sun came up.

Pat Martino was the guitarist in his band. I agreed to play in this band and we made a record called "Bar Wars," but we never did any more records for him. Something went down—I don't know what—and I never heard from him anymore. But it was interesting because he said it was the best record he ever made.

Touring vs. Recording

As sidemen we would only get the fee that we would agree upon before the date. Sidemen on records don't get royalties—they don't get nothing other than the fee that they get doing the recording—unless they have songs that are on the recording.

I always made between three and five times union scale. Or another arrangement could be that I might decide I want this certain amount of money. It depended on who I was working with. I might say I want $5,000 for a recording date—maybe more depending on the date. But this backfired on me one time.

I had one experience when I didn't want to work for a guy. I thought, I'll ask for this tremendous amount of money and he's just going to say no. I figured he couldn't afford to pay me that kind of money for a record date. So he said what do you want and I told him amount I needed. And he said okay.

It was one of the worst dates I ever did. I had to suffer through the record date because he couldn't play it. He thought it was alright. I thought it was something you could roll up and throw it right into the trashcan. So I never did that again.

That taught me one lesson. I got paid. I got some money. But I never did that again because it made me suffer. I had to suffer through playing this cat's music. Take ten, take fifteen, take twenty. When you play a song that many times, you know what happens? You don't play nothin'. So what I learned from that experience was, when I didn't want to something—I wouldn't do it. Simple as that.

Normally they give me half the money in cash and the other half of the money goes through the union. All the big record companies have a union contract. Half of the money might go through the union and then to get your money you have to go through the union and pay the tax on the money. Then they give you a check. I like to do it like that.

But then the union takes a lump sum out. So then the record company gets slick and they take the taxes out on the whole amount. On $5,000, you might be paying $600 for this and $300 for that, and so forth. Next thing you know, you have just $3,500 left. So I take half the money upfront and then send the other half of the money through the union. That's how making a record works.

Because I was in "Hair" on Broadway for four years and a half, most of the time I never went out on the road with the people who I recorded with. I just did the records. The record would become a hit. Then they could use any musicians in order to get as close to the record as they could. So I would make the hit record and somebody else would do the touring. And that's your touring band.

Most of my stuff was so original these cats couldn't play it. But I moved on to the next level. I kept moving. Along those lines, I'm going to lay the next parts out in sections.

Just as the organ period, the saxophone period and the guitar period overlap, so too does my creative arch at this time. It isn't that I'm only doing one project or artist at a time; rather, these endeavors are all spinning out like spokes. And I'm the hub. And the hub is moving right along because the wheel is in constant forward motion.

Section Six

Hair

West Indian Dances

Richard Tee, Ralph MacDonald, Eric Gale, Chuck Rainey and myself, we used to record a lot in the city. Just for fun—just to blow out some steam—we used to play a lot of these West Indian dances on weekends down the street from the Apollo Theater.

When we used to play cabaret gigs on the weekends, any club or organization could rent the room. And the band came with the clubroom. You had to play music for them to enjoy themselves. At the end of the night they had to be wringing-wet and half-drunk and singing the last song we were playing as they were going out the door. That meant the next week you had another gig there.

Eric Gale played long solos. And the more we played for the West Indians the more they loved it. Everything was up tempo. Not too much slow stuff. As long as they're dancing and sweating, it was cool.

It was great because the job paid $25 per night and my rent was $52. So if I worked one weekend, Friday and Saturday nights, I had the rent money for the month.

There was another bass player named Jimmy Lewis who used to play with us. Jimmy was doing some previews for a play at the Shakespeare House down in the Village.

"Hey man, why don't you come check this out?" he said. "It might play on Broadway."

"Yeah, okay," I said. "I'll check it out."

I went to the Shakespeare House and I saw these kids with long hair in these raggedy pants and it looked like they needed a bath and smelling bad and smoking marijuana—just walking around smoking weed.

"I can't do this," I told Jimmy. "Because I ain't playing with no funky-ass, holes in they pants, ass is out, funky-looking and needing a bath kids."

I ain't never seen nothing like that. That's hobo clothes. That wasn't no shit you be wearing on the street. But I didn't know it was a new trend.

So I left and I never went back. Next time I saw Jimmy he brought it up again.

"Hey man, you did one rehearsal and you never came back. Man, this guy wants you bad," Jimmy told me. "It's going to Broadway."

I said, "Get out of here." I like to wear nice clothes. I've got on a shirt and tie. These kids don't got no shoes on.

"And this is a Broadway play?"

"Yes," he said. "It's going to Broadway."

So I said, "What is it called?"

"Hair."

"What do you mean, 'Hair'? It's all bouffant. Some of these kids, they don't look like they *comb* their hair."

And he says, "It's about hair. Just 'Hair.'"

Hair

The spotlight is on Ronald Dyson. He is standing there on the stage by himself. And the light comes up from darkness. I start playing with my hands on the tom-tom. The same street beat I heard as a kid in New Orleans, I start playing it with my hands to establish a real tribal sound.

"Aquarius—Let the Sun Shine In" is always the first song.

He starts singing and all the rest of the actors come on stage. There are some psychedelic guitar sounds because the first guitar player Steve Gillette turns up his reverb and takes a piece of metal up and down the guitar strings. Sounds like it was coming out of space! This is the beginning of the play.

"Aquarius" has such a nice lope to it that I can't play it with the sticks. So I come in with the street beat playing with my hands; then I go to the mallets.

Jimmy Lewis convinced me to go back for rehearsals again. And then it opened for previews at the Shakespeare House and then next you know they took it to Broadway. I'm the original drummer from "Hair."

Opening night, the end of the first half of the show, they drop a cloth over the kids. The next thing you know, these kids come out of the cloth and they don't have no clothes on. I thought, *Oh God. Look at this.* So I was, we all were, surprised. So I called my wife up.

"Get the lawyer. We're all going to jail. These kids ain't got no clothes on and I think they're going to lock us up tonight."

Then I found out that this was in the show and it is legal to do so long as they don't touch each other. The band performs on the back of a wooden flatbed truck—an actual flatbed truck on the stage—this is the bandstand. It is a part of the scenery of "Hair," this truck, on stage, with the actors.

I'm playing up against the cab of the truck. I play all that music with only the one cymbal and the hi-hat. I couldn't have another crash cymbal because the cab was right there, me sitting on an upturned wooden apple crate, not unlike the beer cases during my first Mardi Gras Day parade in

New Orleans. This is the first time on Broadway for a full band being *on stage.*

Two guitars, bass, three horns, eight pieces total on the bed of a flatbed truck. Four tires on the back, two under the cab, this old-timey farm truck has a canopy over the top that reads: *Fruits and Vegetables,* and me playing the show sitting on an upturned apple crate box.

Hair: Part Two

"Hair" was the play where the people was so free. It was liberating. The lyrics that Jimmy Rado and Jerry Ragni wrote, it took me a year and a half before I understood what they were talking about. Galt MacDermot wrote the music. Michael Butler was the producer. I didn't know what was the story of "Hair." It's got different segments representing many aspects about America at that period.

I was looking at this and I was playing at the same time, but I didn't know how the story line went. And then I learned it and it was kind of incredible, that the story line was kind of deep. On the American system, it changed a lot of stuff in the American culture.

There were segments about different things that were happening: the protest of the Vietnam War, big corporations, the government, the American flag. It was segments about many things that were happening in America.

There was a segment where they talked about the Indians. How we raped the Indians, what we did to them. There was a segment on the Supremes. They used to have these three black girls up on this platform in one dress—all three of them was in this one dress, which was like a stretch dress—and when the lights went down the spotlight cut a silhouette on these girls with this one dress on. The people just burst out laughing—because it knocked them out.

The segment on the flag was where they used to have four guys on each corner of the flag, a guy that would stand in the middle of the flag, and they would sing this song about the flag. This one guy would lie in the flag, and they would swing him. Oh god . . . oh god . . . the audience . . . you could hear a pin drop.

"You son of a bitch. I was in the war. You bastards!"

And we would hear this almost every night because it was the American flag. Then they'd fold it and then they'd put it away.

The next segment was called the Be-In. They had this big can in the middle of the stage with a fire in it, and the kids were like burning draft cards. This one kid came up with this paper flag and threw it in there. Oh shit!

How the kids would rebel. How the rich kids who didn't go to the war went to Canada. How they wore their clothes because they didn't want to wear these Brooks Brothers suits and shit no more, so they wore these jeans with the holes in them.

But I had to play this music that I had created every night. And it had to be better every night. It had to succeed from the previous night, it had to go higher the next night. I was the only cat who could do whatever he wanted.

They used to wrap tobacco up into bamboo papers to make it look like a joint. But I'd be sitting there smoking a joint. I could do whatever I wanted to do. They wasn't going to say nothing. "Don't mess with this guy," Diane Keaton would say. "Because he's controlling the whole show."

Every night they would come out naked. Keith Carradine, who went on to do the Kung Fu program, and his brother are original in the show. Melba Moore is there. There are a handful of us who used that as a springboard. Melba Moore's husband, who was also her manager, would plead with her, "Don't go out there and take your clothes off. My auntie is in the audience. My parents are in the audience," he would plead, him crying in the wings.

We have a dressing room up four sets of stairs. None of the older musicians like to go up there. Alan Fontaine, who was one of the guitar players, and me, it's like our room. Alan and I were the two closest cats in the band. We'd go up there and get high. Before the shows, in between the shows, after the shows. Then we'd be coming down from that play.

Nights I would come down and I would be so tired. I work very hard. I'm inside the music so deeply that some of the things I'll be doing—I don't really know that I'll be doing them. But the energy is there. After four and a half years, I had built that monster up—them forty-three songs—but after I left the show closed inside of six months.

The Economics of "Hair"

A year and about eight months I'm playing the show and in the wintertime I get this bad cold. We called a friend of mine in to play the show. He says, "Where's the book?" So they give him the book and it's all just chord changes: b flat, c minor—thirty-seven pages of chord changes.

Since it's a Broadway play the songs are moving right out there, so for three or four days it was a disaster. So when I came back, Jim Rado, Jerry Ragni, Galt MacDermot and Michael Butler had a meeting with me. They said, *please* write the book out. Or get somebody to write it. Warren Smith is the one guy who could write my stuff out.

"Get us a book," they said. "We'll pay you for it. And we'll have United Artists publish the book." And they did that. So Warren transcribed my drums from the original album we made in the spring of 1968. Actually, we did a series of "Hair" albums. And "Hair" is running now for the last 30 years in Europe. So it still has longevity.

Every week they gave me an extra twelve hundred dollars for my music. Plus I was making thirteen hundred dollars for my pay. I was making $2,500 per week in "Hair." And the band members found out I was making that kind of money. So the musical director tells the guys:

"Leo is the reason why we got a hit show. You're the trumpet player and you're the other trumpet player—and that's great. But the only reason we got a hit is because of Leo. And if anybody goes to the music union, you're fired."

So nobody went to the music union.

I had all of these drummers that was subbing for me. Quite a few drummers: Billy Cobham, Alphonse Mouzon, many drummers I had to teach. Many other drummers came but they never came to play the show. Bernard Purdie came to see the show but he never sub'd for me. I think it was too strong for him.

Once some of the other drummers saw it, they thought, *no, I couldn't do this.* That's the simple form. They never said it to me, but I knew. I can see the cat would be looking at the book—and something else is happening on stage—and so I'd be playing something that's not in the book because I played whatever I wanted to play. Every night.

I never play what is in the book. I'm playing a lot of rhythms that I'm just making up on the spot, something that will go with the song and what's happening on stage—something that will move it and make it go someplace.

I'm doing great. I'm playing at night on Broadway. And I'm recording by day at Rudy Van Gelder's studios. I need to get more space and buy myself a wagon because LaLa is pregnant with our second kid.

So I move the family out of the two-room apartment and get me four rooms, which is right up the street between Columbus and Amsterdam on the Upper West Side. It was big time, man.

Four Room Apartment

In the mornings before I went to work in the studios I pop out the door at 134 West 82nd Street, apartment 4B, with a baby carriage. Quite often I run into Jimmy Garrison taking his son for a stroll. Two black men pushing baby carriages up Broadway? We'd laugh about it. It was unusual because you would just see ladies with strollers.

Jimmy Garrison is a very friendly guy. He is John Coltrane's bass player. So with these kids laughing, crying, and banging on their baby strollers, we have the youngest rhythm section on parade on the Upper West Side.

The rent is $175 per month rent. We have four rooms: living room, dining room, two bedrooms, kitchen, and a bath—that's called a four room in New York City. I have a color scheme happening at this apartment. I painted the walls of the whole apartment pink. Then in each room, I painted the ceiling the same color as carpet.

In one room we had a purple carpet on the floor and so now it has a purple ceiling. Then in the next room we have a red carpet so I painted the ceiling red. If I bought a new sofa or chairs, then I'd paint the apartment again to match the furniture. It was unique because I had this contrast of color happening at this apartment.

As a builder and interior decorator in New Orleans, my father ran a crew of designers for a successful company called Gallaghers. And to earn spending money as a kid one of the things I did between playing gigs with the Nevilles was to work on that crew for my dad. And remember I also worked on a crew with my brother Sydney and Uncle Henry. That's how I became an expert painter.

The landlord in this building, when he wanted to show an apartment to rent, he would call us up and ask could he hold an open house in our apartment.

I'm practicing during the day and I hear this *tap, tap, tap* on the floor underneath the apartment. It's coming up from the apartment beneath us. It is Jack DeJohnette. Jack lives in the apartment under me. He hears something I'm playing that he likes and he grabs his broomstick and starts poking up at his ceiling.

"Keep playing. Keep playing, man."

Sometimes Jack would call me on the phone because he liked what I was playing. I'd say I'm tired. I've got to work tonight. I've got to stop.

New Volvo Wagon

I bought a brand new 1970 Volvo station wagon. Paid cash for that. Cash. Brand new one. You know the smell of a new car? On a Friday I went to the car dealership.

"Here's $500. I want that car," I tell the salesman. "And put a rack on the top."

He said, "That will be $85 more."

I had money up the gazoo in the bank. I gave him $85 more to put a rack on it because I'd be traveling. I wanted to tie stuff to the top. The guy didn't really think I was coming back with the rest of the payment so he gave me a price of $3,500 for this new station wagon.

I come back on Monday to get the car and the salesman is acting like he doesn't want to see me. I have the paper in my hand and I'm trying to catch him. He's going here and he's going there. So I just sit down and wait until he stopped running away from me. Another guy at the dealership came by.

"Mister, can I help you?"

"Yeah, I put a down payment on a car on Friday. I came to pick it up."

He said, "What kind of car?"

I showed him the paper. He's looking at it and he sees the salesman's name on it.

"He sold you this car?" he asked me. And I said yes. Then he turns to the salesman and asks him the same question, "Did you sell this man this car?" Then he turns back to me. "Do you have the money with you?" Then he turns to the salesman, "Go get this man's car."

He brought the car up to the front of the door. And this guy in the middle, asking all the questions, he was the boss. So he takes me in the little room they had and he writes out the paperwork and I gave him the money. He said thank you very much. Here's your title, owner's manuals, got the plates on it. Everything's okay. But I noticed it didn't have the rack on it.

"What happened to the rack?"

And he looks down on the paper and it shows $85 paid for the rack. So he asks the salesman, "Where's the rack?" You're a donkey's ass—that's the nice version—he says to the salesman. And the boss gives me $85 back for the rack.

So now I have a brand new Volvo station wagon. Because I was one of the few guys that had a wagon I could carry a lot of people. But that rack would have come in handy, too.

Sundance

The choreographer of "Hair" is also doing another play right across the street. It is called "The Indians." She liked my music a lot so she asked me to come across the street and see if I could do anything to make it move. There was this piece called "The Sundance."

A Sundance is a dance that the Indians do when they're going to war—they would do this Sundance in preparation for going to war, because they're getting ready to go—and they build a fire and they dance around it. Because you couldn't have a fire on the stage they made lights like the sun, made different colored lights and they have their war costumes on and they would dance.

She choreographed this dance and asked me to make up the rhythms. I watched the rehearsal and I came up with the idea of having a street bass drum, like a band bass drum, turned over on its side. Then I took two sixteen inch floor tom toms and I tuned them up. I used these three drums to make up the rhythms to their dance.

When the play opened I had to rehearse two drummers to play the one part that I played by myself. I had to have two drummers to do that. And I taught them this. The play didn't last too long, though. Now if I would have been over there playing then it would have lasted a little longer.

In "Hair" I was listed in the program guide as the drummer. In "The Indians," right across the street, I had my name in there as the Percussive Consultant. The benefit was that it allowed me to work both plays at the same time. I was burning the candle at both ends, man. Plus I was doing all the records as the session drummer for Blue Note, Prestige, CTI and Kudu Records, too.

I knew the moment was near when I would find myself at the professional and personal crosshairs of my life. I was at the end of my rope with "Hair." And this thing was still haunting me about leaving my first wife.

Friends of mine would see me sitting in the dressing room with my head down. I was never drinker. I never liked alcohol because I had seen my relatives drinking, and I didn't like the taste of it. So I wasn't drinking alcohol but I was sad. Sometimes you have money, success, and everything you think you want in life. But you're still unhappy. So I was searching, and that's when Islam came in.

I needed to get out of Broadway, out of the city of New York, and out of the country.

Section Seven

The Seventies

Becoming Idris Muhammad

I go into the church and I light some candles. One day I meet this man who apparently thinks I am Muslim because I am wearing a beard. And he sees this sadness in me and so he explains to me about Islam. How it would help me to regenerate my life because I am sad about my wife and what was happening and I am really down. So this man explains Islam to me and one thing leads to another and him saying that maybe my life will be changed.

Then a Sunni Muslim friend of mine showed me the Quran. As I went to pick it up he told me that I couldn't touch it until I had performed a Wudu. Wudu is the cleansing of one's face, neck, hands and arms up to your elbows, rinsing out one's mouth and wiping one's feet clean so that the contents of what you read can penetrate to one's soul. So I did that. And it did change my life. I read up on the Muslim faith and it changed my life. And this all has stayed with me.

And the next thing you know, my connection with the Creator becomes close. My connection between me and my Lord is direct. I decided if I was going to do this, I am going to do it all the way. That's when I stop using my original name.

I am transformed.

The man suggested to me my Muslim name. I worked with it and came up with Idris Muhammad. But I had already made a lot of records under the name Leo Morris. One businessman is telling me that if I change my name I am going to have a problem because no one will know that Leo Morris and Idris Muhammad is the same guy. But I think, *well, if I stay the same person then people will know that it's me.* And it worked like that. I was performing in Europe when this guy comes up to me.

"There used to be the only guy who could play like that was Leo Morris. Now you're the guy! But what happened to Leo Morris?"

"It's me," I had to tell him. "Leo Morris and Idris Muhammad is the same guy."

The second record I did with Lou Donaldson on Blue Note Records is "Mr. Shing-A-Ling" in 1967. During these sessions, Frank Wolff is the first guy that called me Idris correctly. We were talking at Rudy's studio and he asked me:

"What is your name now? *Idris?*" He repeats Idris in his German accent. Equal emphasis on both syllables; both syllables rhyme with "peace." "I like Idris," he says.

I changed my life when I became Muslim and from that day until now I have always been successful. I have been in a lot of pain. I had been in a lot of trouble. My first wife had left me and I was searching for something to pull me out of this rut. I had become a junkie. I was a *neat*, which means that really nobody knew. I was a clean junkie. I wasn't around a lot of people who were junkies.

But the trumpet player Lee Morgan discovered me at a dealer's house one time and confronted me. When I told him about the heroin, he cursed me, grabbed me, shook me, and then threw me in the shower and blasted me with cold water. Then I went home and stayed inside my house for a week.

Cold turkey. I got hold of myself. I could think more clearly and I felt better about myself. I learned about how to treat human beings. And that's one thing out of being a Muslim, I learned how important we are as human beings.

No matter what's your color, where you're from, what your status is or where you live. We are human beings first. And then we are who we are after that. My mother always reminded me that I am a human being. And the people who I am with are human beings. If I were with bad guys I would be tempted to do bad things. So be careful who you are with, she would say. And be careful what you do. If you do something and you have to apologize then check yourself so you don't do it again.

If you do something and it's not good then you have to rectify it. So as you go through life, you keep doing wrong things, you end up dead, you end up in prison, you end up not a good human being. What I did with my life helped me to do this music. How I was raised in my family's house. Because my life is separate from my music.

Islam is not so much a religion as it is about each person as a human being. The whole thing is about the connection between you and your Lord. I know when I'm not right. I know when I'm not speaking right. I know when I'm not thinking right. I know myself.

I remember the day I became Muslim and from that day I have always been successful. It's about you as a human being—whatever your religion—you've got to go before the Creator on the Day of Judgment. So when you go before the Creator, and you have your book of deeds, the Creator is going to be reading from your book—not from mine, not from my religion.

So I learned a few things by being around some nice people and I learned how to perfect myself as a good human being. My spiritual progression took a huge leap when I left New York for Saudi Arabia. Every Muslim, at least once in his life, makes Hajj. I had been a Muslim for several years before I first made Hajj in 1970.

Kissing the Blackstone

It's quiet outside. It's peaceful. The sky is changing into colors from black with stars above like you can't believe. This is a dramatic and stark contrast to New York City. As the sun dances up, the sky begins to radiate and it becomes the prettiest color of blue.

At dawn you walk around the Ka'bah seven times. In Mecca the Creator's throne is right over the Ka'bah. That started the race. *That's a lot of house.* The Ka'bah is the first worship place that was built in the world for the Creator.

When you go there and circle the Ka'bah it's called making Tawaf. And since every Muslim makes Hajj—every one visits the Ka'bah, and then proceeds to make Tawaf. At the end of this cube-shaped building called the Ka'bah the Creator sent down a stone that was the color white.

In order to draw all of the bad stuff out of your heart, you kiss the stone. And the stone would turn black. It's called a Blackstone. By kissing the Blackstone, all of the bad sins come out of your heart.

After people make the Hajj their face is radiant. It has life. It has lightness because you have no blackness in your heart. So people who do a lot of bad things, it reflects in their face. You understand? You look at a person and you can tell—this guy is messed up; or this lady is messed up—because their face isn't radiant.

I interact with a lot of people because I'm a human being. But if people really know me—even when I'm not around them—then they see my program. Then they know what I've been doing. How did I accomplish this? If it wasn't with the help of the Creator—how did I accomplish what I accomplished? How did I come up off that street with the shells on it and end up being the guy that I am today?

They might wonder how I could do this. But I'm not special. I'm just a person who loves the Creator. And due to that, I'm able to do a lot of good things. There was a great period in my life when I progressed spiritually.

And my spiritual progression made my music progress. So many things came through that period.

Every time I go to Mecca, it seems like the first recording I do upon my return is a hit record for them. Whoever I come into contact with, they have a hit record. This was my first of five trips to make Hajj in Saudi Arabia.

The Contractor

Back in New York. Time to meet with the contractor of "Hair." Time to get situated back on Broadway. The contractor is the guy who contracts the musicians to play in each theater. When there's a play they give the hiring to a contractor. He goes around and hires all the musicians who he thinks could do this particular job.

The contractor can fire and hire any musician in that theater. He'll come around when the show starts, make sure everybody's there, maybe listen to fifteen or twenty minutes of the show, then he splits. He's off to the next theater, seeing if everybody is on that job.

"Hair" had many performances going on around the country. I would go to Los Angeles, show the drummer there how to play. Go to Chicago and show that drummer how to play. I'd go around at every Grand Opening of "Hair" and show the guys how to play the show. So that opened up a whole new avenue for me, being on Broadway and instructing everybody that was not on Broadway. It became a cottage industry for me. But it was always putting me under too much stress.

I was my own boss in "Hair." It was unusual that a drummer could have this much clout in a play on Broadway. I had the say-so to what I wanted. I could play anything I wanted. Anything. No other drummer could do that. And they were very kind to me. But there came a day when I had had enough of Broadway.

I was doing a lot of recording at this time. It was Ralph MacDonald doing percussion, Richard Tee on keyboards, Eric Gale on guitar, Chuck Rainey on bass and me on the drums. We was the guys recording in town. About this time we went to do a tour with the CTI All-Stars Band. I hadn't quit "Hair" yet, but I was trying to figure out how to disentangle myself from it.

At the CTI concert in Detroit, Michigan, is where I met Roberta Flack.

"I need this drummer," she said. "I got to have you in my band"

And I told her I am still with "Hair."

"Whenever you quit 'Hair,' I want you in my band," she said.

I was at the end of my rope with "Hair." I needed to get out of Broadway and out of the country. Two close friends of mine had booked tickets for me to return with them to Saudi Arabia. I had no idea where this would take me. I had no idea that returning to Mecca and Saudi Arabia was only the first stop.

Ancient Drums

I returned to Saudi Arabia in 1973. Because my friends booked the tickets, I had no idea until we got here that they had also booked tickets for Sudan and Egypt. We made Hajj together in Mecca. Mecca in Saudi Arabia is strictly a religious place. There is no other business inside of there. Outside of Mecca, that's where the people raise their horses; that's where you might see Arabian stallions and so forth. This trip has three legs to it. After Saudi Arabia we head for Sudan by airplane.

When we arrive in the town in Sudan there is an evening religious ceremony in progress. The sky is striated from oranges and reds to the color of torn plums. I can hear the sound of these drums. People are dancing. They are having a party. People are having a good time. And this goes on all night. The drummers have the energy to play the drums like that.

They play until dawn just before the Morning Prayer, the Fajr Prayer, which is the first of five daily Muslim prayers, about an hour and a half before sunrise. Then they stopped playing. Silence. A herd of gazelles rushes over the plains.

Sudan is a huge country on the continent of Africa. Its name means, "Land of the Blacks." It's an ancient place. The drummers there are very important. The drummers are highly respected. The king needs drummers for all his celebrations. If you play the drums you're the messenger. The drums are really powerful in Africa.

The drum in Africa is the communication line. They don't have Western Union. I remembered as a kid in New Orleans how I could hear my brother's drum clear over to where my sister's house was. How high the pitch was determined how far the sound carried. The higher the pitch the farther it travels. I made this connection again when I reached Sudan.

I saw things that reminded me of being in the country with my dad as a kid growing up in the South. And all these fragments of my life became connected because I could relate what I was experiencing in Sudan in 1973 with what my dad was trying to show me by leaving the city of New Orleans with him and going into the countryside in Mississippi when I was a kid.

There was no caste there of white colored Africans, brown colored Africans, black colored Africans. They were just Africans. And the people were so beautiful and so kind. And they treated each other so kindly. The women had hair like Shirley Temple, but it was black. They were so pretty. They were so surprised that we were Muslims from America. They had never met another Muslim who was born in America.

"How many wives do you have?"

We said, "We only have one wife."

"No, you got to have more than one wife because you got to have lots of children—lots of children to carry on your bloodline."

"That don't work in the States," we told them.

But the women get along here because they are raised like that. They explained how it is actually better for you to have more than one wife. Because you are going to have more than one woman anyhow, they said, so if you have more than one wife then you can spend time with all of them without jealousies. But you have to treat each one equal. Whatever you give one, you have to give the others.

When I told them I was a drummer, they told me the story of how years ago the king's hut was always next to the drummer's hut. The drummer lived well because his house was next to the king. And every time they want something done, they called for the drummer.

If the king took another wife, they announced with the drum that there would be a party. Saturday night, the cat would call over on the drum and tells everybody, Come on man, there's a party over here. If the king has a new baby, the drums send the telegram. The celebrations are announced on the drums.

And when the message was sent, then they sent the message back. Call and response. The drums do that. And when the king's relatives come to visit then the drummers play for the party. And the party is all night long. The drummer has to play all night long.

But the next day, he was rewarded for it. Maybe he might want another wife, or might want a cow or something. He was living great because he was the drummer. This was the tradition.

So the drummers would ask us, "You all live good? How many wives you got?

As they explained their tradition to me they made it clear that the drummer always had the highest standard over the other tribesmen. He always had rank over the warriors and others because the village depends upon him to send the messages. And to be able to send and receive the messages you have to understand the language of the drum.

Drummers are sharers. The only way you can learn is from other drummers. Listening to them; playing with them—that's the only way that you can learn the drums. From the old days of African drumming—that's where that comes from. Drummers always share with other drummers. I learned a lot about drums and drumming in Sudan. I began incorporating the sound of many drummers into one guy on one drum set.

I had the most marvelous time I ever had in my life in Sudan, them trying to give us wives and everything. And the water in Sudan, oh my goodness gracious, the water was sweet—it tasted like crème soda. I had a big barrel with a cover on it, and I went and got some water and that tasted like crème soda. That's water that comes from the Nile. No wonder the pharaohs wanted to rule from Egypt.

When we were leaving, all the people from one guy's family came down to see us off. We thought it was all the people from the village, but it wasn't but just this one guy's family! Others arrived to see us off too. It was so beautiful. But I couldn't take it because it would have done more harm than good. So I left it alone. I sucked it up and came on back home to America.

My traveling companions Lukmon and Ababukar and I didn't want to leave Sudan. But Ababukar knew some policemen in Egypt he wanted to see. We were headed for Egypt.

I saw the Blue Nile and the White Nile. Boy, was that beautiful. We spent two weeks in Egypt. Standing on this bridge seeing the Blue Nile and the White Nile in the land where the pharaohs ruled.

We saw the Sphinx and all the pyramids. A lot of people just look at it as the Sphinx and see it as this lioness with a woman's head. But that area is graveyard because it is the burial ground of the Pharaoh. Oh my goodness, I didn't like that at all. It was kind of creepy for me because it was in the graveyard.

After spending two weeks in Egypt we headed home for America. It was four months we were gone. I especially enjoyed my time in Sudan. I had to go back to work for "Hair."

Roberta Flack

I'm refreshed, spiritually revitalized, focused on a new sound concept, which I'll explain a little later. I stood a few months in "Hair." The conversation I had before I left for Saudi Arabia, Sudan and Egypt with Roberta Flack in Detroit was resonating in my ears. *"Whenever you leave "Hair," I want you in my band."*

One day I determined to unbraid myself from "Hair" once and for all.

"You can take this job and shove it. I ain't never coming back here again." That's what I told the biggest contractor of Broadway. "Man, I ain't never gonna do this shit no more. Never!"

Roberta had waited four months for me to come back to record with her. She waited four months, man! That's rare for somebody to wait for you to return in the music business. One the one hand, I didn't really believe it was going to happen. On the other hand, when you go to Saudi Arabia and you ask for something, the Creator gives it to you.

Roberta had a record date that she held open for me during my sojourn through Saudi Arabia, Sudan and Egypt. She had slated the recording dates, but I already had the trip out of the country planned.

Then she waited another several months while I finished up with "Hair" and touring with the CTI All-Stars Band. I had a few days off and she flew me into New York. Alphonse Mouzon was sitting in for me, so to speak, not working for her, but filling in for me on the record date. That's the way the cookie crumbled.

"Killing Me Softly" has a Bob Marley feel to it. It was based on something Eric Gale was playing in the studio. That one chord on the first beat—the open note on the "one"—that was just something Eric was playing around with in the studio. Roberta heard that and she put those lyrics to it.

"Killing Me Softly" goes double-Platinum in 1973. We toured with her extensively to promote it. In 1975 we returned to the studio to do the album "Feel Like Makin' Love."

When I returned to New York from Sudan I changed my drum sound. I brought in all this bottom end. This is when I added the second floor tom and second ride tom. And when I changed my set up it provoked me to try something different in my playing. I started playing different rhythms.

I played the rhythm of the song "Feel Like Makin' Love" on the two floor toms. I didn't want the size of the drums to make the tones. That's why both my ride toms are the same size. And both my floor toms are identical in size to each other. I control the tone and the pitch with my special tuning process. It's African sounding tuning, a tight snare with the toms singing.

We're in the studio. I put on the headset. The left one is on the ear, the right one is out—pushed back behind my right ear. I can hear through it—but it's not over my ear. That way I can hear the drums and cymbals naturally in one ear and hear the musicians coming through the headset in the other ear. So I have a balance.

I can't hear the cymbal like I want to with the headset covering both ears. The headset destroys the sound of my cymbals: it's artificial, it's smothered. I don't feel it and hear it natural through the headset. So I wear one just slightly behind my right ear and one on my left ear. I need to feel the touch of the cymbals in my hand and hear it too. My left ear is a better ear for hearing. My monitor is always on the left side. Got my headphones set and by now I've already got the concept of the song.

I'm hearing Roberta sing: "*That's the time, I feel like makin' love to you.*"

And Gene McDaniels says, "This is the first song she's going to record."

I'm thinking this is really nice. The rhythm to "Feel Like Makin' Love" is based on something I'm hearing Chuck Rainey playing on the bass. I'm hearing this bass line and I'm thinking of what to play with this.

I pick up the mallets. It doesn't sound like a stick song. And I hear Eric Gale playing the chord changes on guitar.

And the group says: "Let's stop. Let's stop. Let's record it. Let's record it."

"Feel Like Makin' Love" was done in one take.

Special Tuning Process

My drum playing is very personal to me. You can always hear my drum playing because my special tuning process—both drums and cymbals—is unique to me. There's a lot more to it that what might be apparent to the casual listener. By starting with the tuning of the drums and then matching that tuning across the cymbals, I can make the band sound very good.

I've got my drums set up a certain way so when I go into a club or concert hall all I have to do is turn a few lugs in order to get the drum sound that I want in that particular club or auditorium. I start the tuning with the deepest floor tom and work back to the snare drum with the snares turned off. You can hear the intervals, but it's not to specific notes. A piano player might say, this is A or this is F. But it's really just tuned at the key of Idris.

I want to play the drum the way I want to play it, which starts with the tuning process. I have the bottom heads tighter than the batter side. So when I adjust the top heads I like the drum to ring. A lot of my students, I'm showing how to get three pitches out of one drum.

How you start from the rim, and you go a couple of inches further, then in the middle of the drum: there's three different pitches in each drum. But you've got to know how to play them to get this particular thing out.

You'll never hear another drummer who has his drums and his cymbals tuned in the same intervals as mine. When they make my cymbals for me I have them tuned to my drums. Which is unusual. So another aspect of my special tuning process is that the cymbals are tuned with the drums.

I want to play chord changes, sustain pedal—like the piano player has. I want to hear the drum ring. I want you to hear the changes when the changes are changing from the chorus to the bridge; I want you to hear that in my drum set. I want to be able to move while the song is moving.

Initially, I really didn't know where my concept came from. I hadn't thought too much about it until my older brother Weedy heard me playing. Weedy and I were talking and he told me where this concept came from.

My dad was a banjo player. He used to play the banjo and sing to us in the house. I learned melodies and block chords from just listening to my dad sing and play rhythms on the banjo. As a kid, when Weedy would come home from the road, Dad would sing to us.

All the songs which I would later learn were standards, I had thought my dad had written them. For instance, I thought my dad had written "Stella by Starlight." And it wasn't until I moved to New York that a guy informed me that these tunes were called standards. So my musical concept of lyrics and rhythm and chord changes and melodies came through me like that. My dad had the rhythm of playing the banjo.

I like to play with singers to support how they sing their lyrics. Singers love me to play with them because I play so close to their lyrics that it is easy for them to sing. That's why a lot of singers like for me to play behind them.

So that's part of my experience with the drums: tuning and playing musical drums. Other guys don't think about it this way.

And I am the drummer? Normally the guitar player will do this. Or the piano player. But a drummer can play something that makes me sing this well? It's because I play the melody of the song that the singers like me to play with them. Roberta Flack loved my playing so much that we never wanted to part.

My brother Weedy brought to my attention that I applied all this to the drums.

India: 1975

I had been with Roberta for a couple years when I took some time off and went to India in 1975. I was there three months and a half so I observed a lot of things, man. I noticed some similarities between what was happening there and what had happened in New Orleans. India broke off a part of itself and Pakistan was established. And then Bangladesh broke off from Pakistan and formed its own country. This reminded me of what was happening in New Orleans.

When India was just India there was a caste system over there because the British ruled it. The British army soldiers had different colored complexions than the Indians. And the soldier compared himself a little bit better than one who wasn't a soldier. That was like down here in New Orleans. You have black guys from New Orleans; then you have the Creoles who mixed with white people. So that put a caste system in America. And that's what happened to India.

Muslims who lived in India wanted their own state. And they got their own state. And then the brothers who was from Bangladesh, they lived near the water, they were darker complexioned and they went to fight with Pakistan so they ended up with their own state, which is present day Bangladesh. So there aren't any Muslims left in Pakistan. The Muslims are in Bangladesh.

I was in New Delhi when my Visa expired so I took a train to Bombay because they wouldn't renew it in New Delhi. But I got an extension for three months in Bombay. And I went to Agra to visit the Taj Mahal.

The Taj Mahal is comprised of all marble. Them guys built that place in the jungle. Because it is all marble, the builders were expert carvers. They carved it out of the jungle and then they carved it out of white marble. It took them over 20 years and 20,000 people to do that. And it took over 1,000 elephants, too.

Shah Jahan built that for his wife because he loved her so much. He was going to build another one for himself out of all black marble. But his sons thought he was squandering too many resources and too much money so they overthrew him.

A lot of their coins were made out of aluminum. You could throw it on the ground and it didn't even ring. And the paper money was made out of such bad paper that when it got old it just withered away in your hands.

Bangalore is the city where they make the bangles for the ladies. You could buy a box of these glass bangles for a dollar. It was a time when I could reach back in my mind and remember the trinkets being thrown at the ladies and the young girls at Mardi Gras in New Orleans. Then we're seeing cows as we're walking down the street. If a cow pokes his head in your door, you're supposed to give him something to eat. Boy, that was something to see. Especially for me. It was really wonderful to be able to be in those places at that time, when things weren't as modern as they are today.

We had lunch inside the Taj Mahal. We would eat on a dosti matt. Dosti means friend and connotes friendship. The dosti matt is a piece of cloth that you set down on the floor. We didn't eat at a table with chairs. We sat on the floor and it was cool in there because of the marble. We had a siesta every day because it was too hot to do anything. We just stayed inside and chilled. Then we took a nap in there. I slept like a baby.

Rosebud Studios

A lot of drummers in New York City like what I'm doing. They'll come by when I'm playing a gig to listen to my playing. All these guys were telling me how much I was influencing their drum playing. But recording is a more private affair.

There was one incident at Rosebud Studios in midtown Manhattan when I agreed to let another drummer come into the studio while I was recording. I was recording at Ralph MacDonald's studio when Ralph approached me.

"This guy, he likes you. And he'd like to come in and watch you work."

"Well maybe it might not be a good idea."

And he says, "Well look, how about if he just comes in to the engineer's room."

So they guy comes in. I'm recording three takes—three or four takes—and then I go into the engineer's room and I meet him.

"Oh man, I love your playing, and I really admire your work."

"Great," I say. "I'm very delighted to meet you. What is your name?"

And he says, "My name is Steve Gadd."

This was the beginning of Roberta having two drummers on the same album. Steve and I have been friends for many, many years now. Not only drummer friends, but real heart friends; friends that you love and respect as human beings. Even so, I have suggested to Steve that just because you play black drums and endorse black drum sticks—that don't make you black. We had a laugh.

Also Bernard Purdie and Alphonse Mouzon, who worked with Roberta before and after me, these guys are my dear friends. When Bernard Purdie, who was playing the drums for Aretha Franklin, came by "Hair" he heard this unique open hi-hat technique I told you about. Next thing you know, Bernard had put it on Aretha Franklin's "Spanish Harlem" record.

"Look Idris," Bernard told me, "I stole this from you."

But today's younger drummers don't share in the way we did. Now guys are personal and guarded about their work. Everybody's hiding stuff that don't even belong to them. I was making up these rhythms and doing these things, not knowing what I was doing. It never dawned on me what I was doing—that I was trendsetting.

After about four years of recording and touring with Roberta, I had had enough. "Killing Me Softly" was killing *me*. When it came time for me to leave Roberta, her manager brought me all of my drums except for the two natural blonde maple Gretsch tom-toms I added when I started with her.

When you was working for Roberta you could just go somewhere and charge it to Roberta. And when Roberta fired me one time, the last time it turns out, her roadie had put the wrong drums in the cases. So they accidently took my original Slingerland natural blonde ride tom and gave me the same size Gretsch drum instead. They took the wrong drum.

I think she still has those two drums—my original Slingerland ride tom and the Gretsch floor tom. I'm tempted to ask her for the Slingerland tom back, but because she paid for two drums I think she kept two drums.

Philosophy of People

If you watch a person who is sleeping you will understand what he will look like when he's dead. Some look like they're already dead.

Dead. Dead. Dead.

You see people who made other people suffer here on earth. You can see that in their face. There's darkness in their face. You look at a person and you can see this guy is messed up or this chick is messed up because their face isn't radiant.

If I know of a person like that I just talk to them for a while and then I kind of ease away. That's because I have a one-strikeout formula. If people do anything that touches my heart against me or hurts me, then I don't fool with them no more. I give them one strike and they're out. The ballgame is three strikes and you're out. But I don't give you three strikes. I give you one chance.

On the other hand, I've seen people who have passed on but they look in death great because they had a great life. You can tell when a Muslim goes to Mecca because their face is radiant.

We're all trying to obey the Creator and do things with our lives. But there are people who do more wrong things than good things. And you can feel it. You can see it and you can feel it.

There are people in Pakistan, India, they'll shake your hand and then they grab the thumb. There's a special person on the earth, who the Creator put here, and he has no joint in his thumb. His thumb can rotate. So when a Pakistani shakes your hand they might try to see if your thumb can rotate. They're looking for that special person. But only the Creator knows who that is.

If you come into contact with him by chance then there are big blessing for you because you've touched him. He could be here in New

Orleans—makes one step, be in New York. I've been around a lot of heavy, heavy spiritual people. I've been taught a lot of things.

So people who reflect goodness, it comes out in their body, it comes out in their face. You can see it. If you shake their hand, you can feel it in their handshake. We're all trying to obey the Creator and do good things with our lives. But there are people who do more wrong things than good things. And you can feel it. You can see it and you can feel it. You understand?

Creed Taylor and the Origin of CTI Records

Creed Taylor is a famous producer. Producing at the time for A&M records and having signed Wes Montgomery to the label, Creed is responsible for producing many of Wes Montgomery's hit records. Wes Montgomery died. And Creed decided to leave A&M records.

Creed began getting all of the top artists in town and this is how he formed his own label, Creed Taylor International—CTI Records. This is when Creed brought George Benson to CTI records.

We're at Rudy Van Gelder's studio recording the "The Other Side of Abbey Road" record. Ron Carter was asking me how much money I was getting for the date.

"Herbie and me are getting five times scale," he tells me.

Not knowing that you've got to ask for the money, I say I'm getting three times union scale for this record.

Ron says, "You can't just accept what they give you. When they call you for the gig, you've got to tell them what you want. You're doing the same date we're doing so I think you should talk to Creed.

After we cut "You Never Give Me Your Money," Ron came over to the drum booth and he asked me, did I talk to Creed about the money? So he said:

"Hey, Creed. Idris wants to talk to you." And he came over.

"Ron and them is getting five times scale," I said. "And I want the same thing."

And he said, "Okay."

And that was it. That's how I got to elevate myself.

I had been making three times union scale. That's how I got to five times. I learned you had to ask for it.

"The Other Side of Abby Road" was the first record George Benson did for CTI. I was making a lot of dates for Blue Note records and Fantasy at this time. In fact, two years prior I had worked with George Benson on the "Alligator Boogaloo" date with Lou Donaldson for Blue Note Records.

Now I was the house drummer for Prestige. I was the hottest cat in town. I was the guy. So they called me to do dates for CTI, too. This all actually began when I was working on Broadway doing "Hair." I was recording by day and performing "Hair" every night.

Herbie Hancock, Ron Carter and I were the basis of these recording sessions. We were the original foundation of the CTI musical concept. With Herbie Hancock on the keyboards, Bob James was brought in by Creed to score the music. Herbie Hancock was creating the music and Bob James would work from that template.

But this arrangement caused Herbie to quit from doing dates with Creed because the voicing of Herbie's chords were being used to orchestrate the songs to make it sound like the whole band—strings, horns, everything—was there when the recording was happening.

Bob James would take the music and he would score in a big band. That's when Bob James started playing for Creed. This is when I met Bob James. So then it became me and Ron Carter and Bob James. Together we became the session men for Creed Taylor. That's when I became the session drummer for CTI.

Thinking back to my first recording experience at Cosimo's Studios in New Orleans, the dates were done with a total of two microphones. There was just one mic for the singers. And there was only one other microphone, which was placed in the middle of the studio for the band.

Fifteen years forward, to contrast and compare, now we have seven microphones on the drums alone. It was during the Creed Taylor-produced CTI sessions, in collaboration with the musicians, and engineered by Rudy Van Gelder, this is when all the microphones came in.

Homeless Person's Bass Drum

Rudy asked me to come to the studio a couple hours earlier than the other musicians to get the drum sound for "Inner City Blues." I went to the studio and discovered that Rudy had a custom-built drum booth made for me.

Rudy has one mic on the ride tom, one on the floor tom, one on the bass drum, one on the snare drum, two mics on the cymbals and one on the hi-hats: seven microphones. And that was only in the drum booth—which separates the drums totally. We got the drum sound on all the drums and cymbals except he couldn't get a good bass drum sound.

"Idris," he says, "let me cut a hole in the bass drum. I'll pay you for the head."

Rudy cut a hole about the size of a silver dollar in the front bass drum head.

"I'll put a pin mic inside," he says. "Let's put some foam rubber around it and see if we can get a better bass drum sound."

And Rudy did that. That's where the hole in the bass drum comes from. And he did get a nice bass drum sound.

"Listen," Rudy said. "When you come in the engineer's room and you listen to the playback, don't say anything. Just listen."

After that, the guys in the studios in New York would ask me, "Hey man, how did Rudy get the bass drum sound?"

"I don't know, man," I'd say. "I don't really know."

Around this time, Rudy bought himself a set of blue sparkle Gretsch drums. Then he cut a hole about the size of a coffee saucer in the front bass drum head. He had me tune them up for him. But I never recorded on Rudy's drums. I always played my own drums and cymbals at Rudy's.

When you have the mics on the drums, sometimes I've got to tell the engineer to bring my bass drum sound up. Some guys know how to record and how to mix the drums, but some producers don't know. So you have to suggest to them what to do with your drum sounds. Most of the time they respect what I have to say—what I want my drums to sound like on the recording after it's finished.

Now all of the drums that are in the studios and festivals come with a hole in the bass drum head—everybody plays like that. All the jazz cats play like that. So I use a rider that I need a bass drum *without* a hole in the front. I like to hear my drums sing. But that was the trend we started at that time. That's where that came from.

Now what I call a bass drum with a hole in the front—you got pillows, there's a blanket, foam rubber padding—I call it a "homeless person's bass drum." You don't know if they're going to play it or sleep in it.

Inner City Blues

The date starts at ten o'clock in the morning. Everybody's ready, but there's no Hank Crawford. We called his house. We called everyone we could think of. We can't find Hank.

The date for "Inner City Blues" has five horn players. Grover Washington, Jr. is one of the horn players. Thad Jones is arranging this date for Hank Crawford.

"Grover, would you just play the alto on these songs until Hank comes?" Creed says, "And then we'll take you off and put Hank back on."

Grover says, "Great."

The first number we did was "Inner City Blues." We had done an instrumental record for George Benson, "The Other Side of Abbey Road." That was successful so now we were doing "What's Going on" for a Hank Crawford date. That was kind of a formula that Creed was using.

The first number went right. Then we did a couple more. Then we did a couple more. We worked like that for three days and then we stopped on a Wednesday. We come back Monday to begin the date over and at about three o'clock we find out that Hank is in Memphis on some old traffic violations—just some old traffic tickets. But it keeps him from making the date.

A month later, I go into Creed's office to pick up some checks and he shows me this record.

"Look, Idris. We got a hit record."

I said, "*What* is a hit? What do you mean we got a hit?"

And Creed shows me this record. I look at the cover and I'm surprised because it's got Grover's picture on it. This is the beginning of Grover Washington's success. It happened just like that. Grover happened to be in the studio and played the date because Hank is missing.

You can put that record on right now and it sounds like he just made it—timeless—that is to me one of the best records that he ever made.

The Lamb on the Lamb

I moved the family from 134 West 82nd Street to Teaneck, New Jersey, in 1971. We had all our kids in the house. Plus we rented to some exchange students at Fairleigh Dickinson University. It was interesting watching our kids interacting with the kids from Sudan, India, Pakistan and so forth all living in the house together.

But teenagers and the telephone? It was out of control. I had to call the phone company and we crafted a solution. The phone guy comes out and he installs a payphone right inside our house. That worked out great. Put your coins in the payphone and you can call anywhere in the world. And they did.

I had a lamb that I kept in the yard around Hajj time. And one day I was going to sacrifice it in the yard. Come that day, we had to run some errands first so I put the lamb in the garage for safekeeping. I didn't want to leave it in the yard.

When we returned home that afternoon I opened the garage door and the lamb dashed out. I think he was waiting on me, waiting on his big chance. So it was running around the neighborhood and I had to chase it down. Me and my sons, we managed to catch it and bring it back to the garage. It was funny to them but this is a serious matter.

In order to sacrifice it you put the lamb on the ground with the head of the lamb facing east. You give it some water. And then you part the hair by the neck. Before you cut it you make sure the reason why is for the Creator. And that's how you sacrifice it. And then give some away to the neighbors before you cook it. And then you cook the lamb for your family.

Meanwhile, one time—it was another year actually, another lamb—my daughter kind of took a liking to the lamb in the yard. We would have it several days and they would feed it oatmeal. So the day of eating came and my daughter, she liked the lamb so much, it affected her to where she didn't eat meat for a number of years. But that's the story of the lamb on Ramadan.

Bob James' Groove

I knew it was a television show. I knew the name of the show was "Taxi." Bob wrote like that. He had a title; he wrote a song about it. That was his thing. He knew what he wanted and we were to portray that for him. We had to make it happen for him.

He had it down on the paper, but with us taking it and playing like he had it down on that paper—putting ourselves inside of it—the music comes together to make it what it is. The music is about the notes that them cats is playing, that Bob is playing, so I got to get inside of that. I've got to be inside of that.

When Bob wrote this song called "Angela" as the theme to the television show "Taxi," we played exactly what he wanted us to play. Because they were going to play this song as the intro to that program, every time it comes on, he knew exactly what he wanted. So we had to portray it for him. We had to make it happen for him.

That's why that thing is slow. Got a groove. Cats can't play that groove. We be groovin'. All of us be groovin' together. Give me a band that can play that? Can't play that groove! Can't play that, man! That's instant stuff that comes from cats who make music. That's real music.

We recorded in a studio on Eighth Avenue around 53rd Street in New York City. In the studio I'm facing Bob James through the window that separates each musician's section of the studio. We're looking at each other face to face because you want to keep this groove happening.

Bob starts off with the intro; when the band comes in there's a double-downbeat—what's called double-clutching—as I put that song in gear. You can't hear that on the bass drum because the producer edited that off the master tape, but you can hear it on the hi-hat.

You can hear how I mirror the tambourine sounds of the Indians dancing to Mardi Gras in New Orleans on the hi-hat cymbals. This tune is a good example of how I duplicate the bell sound of the tambourine—to make it open up and ring—by using the tip and the shoulder of the drum stick; and working the pedal to capture the essence of the pressing machines at Buddy's Cleaners. My style never changed.

Eric Gale is sitting to my left. Ralph MacDonald is percussion on my right. Eric Gale would get a lope in his head, put his head down and we got it. You ain't thinking about nothing but a groove. You want to keep this groove happening. I was just thinking of the music.

You see, I have a natural ability to play in time. A lot of people didn't play in time. They start off slow and end up fast or start out slow and end up slower. You understand? I've got a natural ability that where Bob sets the tempo, I'm locked in there. Right there. After the first three beats, I'm locked in there. I'm locked in.

You ain't going to get me out. You can pour water on my ass—I'm not going anywhere. Ain't going to move, man. Put a fine lady in front of me—I ain't moving. So that's the other part of making a successful recording: that you don't move the time. And that was the reason of that "Taxi" song being a success. Because the time was, when he started it, it was the same when we ended it.

See I have a groove thing. With kind of slow tempo songs, most guys just fall apart, but I can make it groove so hard. And "Angela" was one of those songs that was slow. It had a feel, had a lope, but I made it groove. That's how you hear my music in the song. No other drummer does that. They may do it now because they learned how to do it from me. It gets fatter, it's fatter, it's fatter. That's my forte.

So I stepped on it. I killed it. It grooved so hard Bob just got up from the piano.

"That's it, that's it, that's it," he says just like that!

It means that you're not going to record that again. They don't do that no more.

Making Hit Records

When you record you can feel music while you're doing it. You can feel that it's going to be a hit. Once you get into it, from the beginning, you can feel this is happening. You can feel it. I can feel a hit record. Cats can feel this. And they take it to another place.

Then you just be biting on it, and chewing on it, and groovin' with it and next thing you know it's over. And you play it back. And when you know it's a hit you keep playing it back. It sounds so good you want to hear it again.

This new shit they're doing—playing eight bars then stop—we never did no music like that. Now the computer is used to loop the drums, they play sound cards and that don't feel worth a shit. Them computer recorders are terrible. These people are cheatin' the music, doing records like that.

We started a record and we did it from the beginning to the end. If the shit didn't groove, we did it over again 'till the shit grooved.

In the history of me recording, no record that I ever did stopped at the bridge, then started at the bridge again. How you going to know where the tempo's at, man? The feeling and shit be all different. It's different, different, everything is different. Can't make no record like that. Only singers do that bullshit. But I've never made a record like that. Never.

Take any of my records, you can listen to the time in any of my records and take a click track and click track along to the records, it's the same time from the beginning of the records until the end. That's what I do. Then they started with this click-track thing.

I remember one day I went to a record date for somebody and they had this thing in my headset: *Click-click-click.*

And I say, "What the hell is that?"

"It's a click-track," they say. "It's a metronome. It keeps the time right."

"Man, turn that shit off. I don't need that clicking in my head."

And sure enough, I worked without it. Where we started the tempo at and where it ends is the same with me. I never used a click track because my timing is so great.

Power of Soul

"Power of Soul" is my greatest record. It's only four tracks. The intensity of the rhythms I'm playing—and how settled, and how swinging, and how hard it grooves—is what makes it. The rhythms are like what I played on Roberta Flack's "Feel Like Makin' Love" or on Bob James' stuff.

I made records that would groove me. Those tunes will cool you out. I hear it today, it soothes my heart because I played that great on it. It will get inside your mind. People have told me that "Power of Soul" has changed their lives.

I was on the road with Roberta Flack and the CTI All-Stars when Creed called me off the road. He wanted a record.

"I want a record, I want a record."

I had a couple of days off so I came in. Called Bob James, Grover Washington, Randy Brecker, Gary King, Joe Beck, Ralph MacDonald to do this date.

"I don't have any songs," I told the cats. "You got anything for me?"

And Bob James says, "Yes. Check this out. 'Piece of Mind.'"

Man that was so nice. Oh, God. That's a great song, man. Great song. It's that groovy. That's the first tune that we did. The second tune was "Loran's Dance," Grover's tune. The third we did was Joe Beck's "The Saddest Thing."

"The Saddest Thing" got some real slick stuff on it rhythm-wise. Slick, slick, slick, slick, slick. When I'm playing with the cross-stick and I double the thing. Play it like it sounds double. It's still the same tempo but I play it like it sounds faster. Now you're getting to what my stuff is about.

"Power of Soul," the Jimi Hendrix tune had so much fire that the record was called "Power of Soul"—it was that powerful. Bob wrote some hip, hip horn parts in there for me. Gary King wrote that arrangement. He just came to me and he said:

"Idris, listen at this."

And I said, "What is *that*?"

And he said, "Jimi Hendrix's 'Power of Soul.'"

I asked if he could write it out. The first three tunes were done in one take. "Power of Soul" was done on the second take. That was the last tune that we recorded on that record date.

I had recorded quite a few records at Electric Lady Studios. East 4th Street, off of Sixth Avenue—the Avenue of the Americas—it's a great studio. All Jimi and them had been down in there, man. It's a good feeling in there. Stevie Wonder was recording his records there.

"Power of Soul" is my *underground* hit—that's what I listen to when I want to listen to me, that's what I listen to. It takes me back to the time when we recorded it. It's my classic record.

On Being a Star

I have been around stars all my life. When I got to stardom I really didn't like it. I didn't like being a star because when stars aren't hot they become sad people. Do you understand?

If they were on the tour and they were hot because they had a hot record the tour was a happy tour. But when they were on tour and the record got cold they became sad people. So I never wanted to be a star. I didn't what to be what these people were. I only wanted to be who I was.

When it was my turn to be a star—when I had the hot record, my own dressing room, police standing outside the door, nobody can come in, police escort when I went outside—I didn't want to be that kind of person. After I started making money from these records, I bought myself this buckskin jacket with fringe hanging down the sleeves.

But sitting in that dressing room alone, police outside the door, it kind of felt like when we were kids in New Orleans and you'd play cowboys and Indians and the guys who were captured got put in the jail inside the boxcars by the railroad tracks. I didn't enjoy it because I just liked to be with the other fellas.

In this time, I take a look back at it and I don't know if I would have changed anything because I didn't care about what people were saying about me. They were saying a lot of good things, but I didn't let it swell my head. Only thing I was concerned about was that I wanted to make a living, take care of the family.

I created a style of drumming, which cats try to copy—many guys copied it—but they never could get it. Drummers took portions of it, pieces of it, just pieces. I can say this now, but I wouldn't dare have said it at that time.

Not that I didn't want to be successful. I wanted to be successful. But I didn't like the stardom thing. I just wanted to be a musician that is humble. I was lonesome in that dressing room in my buckskin jacket and sitting all by myself.

If I was doing the recording or the gig with you, you're going to play some of the best shit you ever played in your life. When I record for you, I try to make a hit record for you. You're going to be happy. I like to make people happy.

Pharoah Sanders

I had met Pharoah Sanders back in the 1960's at a club called Slugs down in the East Village. New York was a friendly town in those days. You could meet a guy and just talk to him. And then all of a sudden he might get a gig and he'd call you. That's what happened with Pharoah.

Pharoah Sanders used to play with John Coltrane. And Trane liked to play off Pharoah's energy. I loved Trane. So I liked playing with Pharoah because Pharoah was the closest thing happening to playing with John Coltrane. I knew Jimmy Garrison and Elvin Jones. So Pharoah was the next best thing for me because I never got a chance to play with Trane.

One difference between Trane and Pharoah is that Trane knew how to play changes. And with Pharoah, it was only one change. So we had to build off that change. Sometimes we had to build off that change for 20 minutes. So I had to think of creative stuff. I made a lot of records with Pharoah.

The first date I did with him was the 1969 gatefold LP called "Jewels of Thought." So that was my introduction to playing jazz. I say "jazz" because I am a funk drummer who had played with a lot of jazz cats.

That was a quite interesting record date because we had two bass players and two drummers. It was fun because Roy Haynes was on the gig. It was my first experience of playing with Roy Haynes. And I was happy with that because Roy liked me. If Roy Haynes liked you then you must have something going, man, especially at this time, just because he was Roy Haynes.

To commemorate the date Roy gave me a little copper tympani. It got flooded in the basement of our home in Teaneck, New Jersey. Too bad, because I always had wanted to fill that up and put some crabs in there, man!

Around 1980, I was doing a week at the Keystone with Johnny Griffin and Ray Drummond when Pharoah says he wants to do a date while I'm in San Francisco. This would become the gatefold, double LP, "Journey to the One." This is album number one for Theresa Records.

"Let's do a record." Pharoah says.

I thought, solid. "$2,000," I say.

He had already sent for John Hicks on piano. Pharoah asked me about this bass player. I told him Ray Drummond was cool. So he says to tell Ray he wants to use him.

Ray Drummond calls me up, says, "Pharoah wants to do a date."

"Yeah?"

"He says he would pay me $800."

I say, "I can get you $1,000."

He says, "If you can get me $1,000, I'll gladly do the date."

"Greetings to Idris" opens the record. It is done in one take. I don't have to play a solo. I am playing what I feel. The second tune is Doktor Pitt, a pseudonym for Allen Pittman, and our homage to the producer of the album for Theresa Records.

As the engineer gets to the mix, it isn't hot enough for him. The toms and bass drum, I don't like. The whole album was a little drier than what we wanted too. So I go to San Francisco and perform the final mixes of "Journey to the One" for Pharoah. I play on it and I also perform the final mixes. That's how that record was done. That record put Pharoah back on the map again.

There is a great guy, wonderful guy, named Allen Pittman. One of the best guys I ever worked with. Allen is a producer for Theresa Records. I'm signed to Fantasy Records at this time. I like Allen so much I do something very foolish.

Fantasy Records and Theresa Records

I'm recording for Fantasy Records in Berkeley, CA, during the day. And I'm mixing Pharoah's "Journey to the One" on Theresa Records in San Francisco at night. Driving each evening on I-80 across the Bay Bridge, smoke a joint between the two toll booths on Treasure Island in the middle of the bay, and on into San Francisco.

I have a great contract with Fantasy but I don't want to do no more disco records at this time. I asked Allen to get me out of my contract with Fantasy Records. Ralph Kaplan's son was the producer at Fantasy. That boy had a carte blanche for me.

But I had told Allen Pittman to get me out of my Fantasy Record contract. I had five years with them making $65,000 for the records and another $60,000 in recordings I had to do on other people's records who were artists inside that company.

I made records for people that sold. I made records for myself that sold records. I made records to sell records, man. The last date I did with Fantasy was a disco record called "Make It Count."

When I first heard that record I was in Los Angeles. I was at a friend's house that had a tremendous stereo system, black glass faceplates and big blue meters dancing with huge JBL wooden catacombs over horn speakers. He put that on and I didn't even know it was my record because they wrote an overture on the front of the first tune.

"That's my record? I didn't record that. Damn!"

So now I'm signed with Theresa Records because Allen helped get me out of the contract with Fantasy Records. They paid me for the last record and I didn't have to record no more for them because I didn't want to do no more stupid disco records.

My first date as a leader on Theresa Records is "Kabsha." "Kabsha" means gentle as a baby lamb. It's named after my daughter. I thought "Kabsha" would be like a John Coltrane record. I wanted to do a jazz record—not a funk record—in order to rebrand myself and chart a new direction. I wanted a fresh start after making so many dance records at Fantasy. Ray Drummond on bass, the horn is Pharoah Sanders on one side and George Coleman on the other and me on drums. But business-wise it ended up being not a good idea.

I only did one record as a leader for Theresa because someone other than Allen Pittman didn't want me to do no more records for Theresa. I only did the one record for them. Another player, who was on the record and who I think owned part of the label—it outsold his records. Pharoah got angry. And I couldn't do another record as the leader of the date for the Theresa label. Then I knew I had made a mistake.

In retrospect, with Ralph Kaplan's son producing at Fantasy, they would have put some money behind him as a producer and helped make me become even more successful at Fantasy. But I didn't want to do no more disco. That's how I came to leave Fantasy Records and join Theresa Records—and get blackballed as the leader, even though I was the top selling artist at Theresa—in one fell swoop.

Paris Reunion Band: Red Vibe and Max Roach

Max Roach, great friend of mine, heard me playing one time on a tour in Europe. I'm playing with a group called the Paris Reunion Band. All of these particular guys who were playing in the band had lived in Paris at one time, with the exception of me. But my mother was from Paris so I guess that was close enough. And we formed this band and called it the Paris Reunion Band.

We have a tour of five concerts with Max Roach opening for us, playing solo drums. I'm sitting and watching Max play every night. Max wanted to know how I maintain that energy. I'm going to tell you, just like I told Max, about the secret of the Chia Seed.

When I lived in New Jersey, the black doctor used to be on the radio: "Cures for Black People." He was taking people in his office. So I went one day with $15 dollars in my hand, like he advertised on the radio program. The cure for sluggishness was chia seeds.

Put some on your hands and drop it in some water. Another friend of mine added some black seeds. It'll kick your ass, he says. Or it'll put a hurtin' on your ass. You'll get a burst of energy after 15 or 20 minutes. But it's all natural. It's not something that will harm you. I've been dealing with these chia seeds for about 30 years now. I keep a bottle in my shoes when I travel. I mix them with black seeds.

As I say, the Paris Reunion Band is doing a tour of Europe and one day I was passing through Venice in Italy, going through the airport when I saw this eyeglass place. Here's another force that I harness. The color Red. It's like an ally to me. I saw these glasses in the display window: lovely pair of nice red glasses. I bought those. And then when we were in Spain I passed by this shop and saw these red shoes, and the guy there said his dad could make some shoes for me.

So I had a pair of these shoes made that I play in: shoes the color red. When I'm working I wear red glasses and red shoes. All the time, when I'm playing, it's a vibe that I got.

It's a vibration. I like red.

Once I had a red set of drums. My wife came to hear me play with Pharoah Sanders and she says, get rid of the red set of drums—you're playing like a maniac. But it's a vibe and I like red.

Now when the Paris Reunion Band is time to go on, Max would be sitting in a chair over in the wing watching me playing. I always had drummers standing in the wings watching me. Sometimes when we didn't have anything to do between shows we'd play the drums.

When I became the house drummer at the Apollo Theater, Stevie Wonder, who was traveling as Little Stevie Wonder at that time, came through with the Motown Review. And we would play the drums quite a bit.

But Max Roach in Paris? Man, I watch him because he's Max Roach. But what is he watching me for? I ask Joe Henderson, the saxophone player, what is Max watching? So I get off the bandstand one night and I walk over to him. We sit and talk.

"Max, why are you sitting in the wings?"

He says, "Man, I'm trying to figure out how you play this stuff. How do you play that funky?"

And I said, "Oh, Max. I could show you."

"Yeah, Idris, show me how you do it. Idris," he says, "your drum playing should be canned and sold in the supermarket—that's how slick it is."

I thought, *okay, maybe he's high, or maybe he's drinking too much, he's just saying something nice.* But then I asked the guys in the band. I said, Max said this about my playing. And Joe Henderson turns to me and says, if Max says it then he meant it.

My heros had been Art Blakey, Elvin Jones and Max Roach. Art and Elvin in New York had encouraged me in the mid-1960s. Now I had Max's endorsement and that meant a lot to me, that Max Roach thought I played that great. That cinched the triumvirate for me.

Groove Elation

I had a Top Five record in 1977, "Turn This Mutha Out." John Scofield is making the road gigs with me. We like each other's playing. John and I have been best friends for many years. It is an interesting touring experience.

I have a tour bus that sleeps ten people and when I tour to promote that record we put that bad boy on the road. But some things are happening on the road and I discover the best way to resolve it is to give it up. The guy who I hired as my straw boss was bad-mouthing me. You have the big boss, that's me. And the second boss down, that's the straw boss. That's a term from way back.

I had seen the problems with the Joe Jones band from the onset of my career. More recently, I had learned from Roberta Flack how much agencies can steal from you. Now here I am, going through the same things myself.

I paid $80,000 cash for the tour bus and I now I have to give it up. The straw boss, who traveled with us for a while, it turns out he is been ripping me off to the tune of $1,000 per night. One night he steps off the bus and he splits for New York. Now I'm left to collect the money and pay the guys, the expenses, and all the bills. I realize I have management problems.

So I go back to New York and meet with him. The result of this is that I end up writing *him* a check for $10,000 to terminate our contract. In so doing, I have to give up the band too. I have to fire the whole band to get away from one person because of the way the contract was written.

Come 1995 and John Scofield is putting a band together and he calls me. I am delighted to come to play in the band. Larry Goldings on organ and Dennis Irwin on bass.

Scofield wrote one tune that sounds just like a tune like Grant Green. All of them cats learned from Grant. Grant was so bad. Not only that, but Grant was funky. Grant Green was George Benson's guru. When we rehearsed his music, John would like to ask me about Grant Green.

"How was Grant Green to play with?"

And I said, "Oh man, Grant Green, he was a sweetheart, and he played so great. Grant used to call me Little Brother. He would say, 'Hey Little Brother, listen at this.' And 'Give me a beat to this; give me a beat to that.'"

One day we went to Kara's Music to rehearse. Another band had been in there rehearsing that morning. The guy in the band that had just left the rehearsal studio had been playing on two snare drums. I just happened to start playing on these studio drums until the other guys got everything ready to start our rehearsal. I was just playing stuff on the two snare drums.

So John says, "Idris, what was that!"

I said, "What was what?"

"What you were playing on the two snare drums."

"Well, I was just trying to work something out."

He said, "Keep the two snare drums."

So that day we went to rehearsing, I have two snare drums. One snare drum is pitched to where I typically play it and the other snare drum set up on the left of it is pitched higher. So you have the two different pitches because I'm playing two different snare drums at one time.

The record is so slick. It's such a great cooking band. But I didn't actually hear the record until a year later because we were traveling and everything. As part of the tour, the band goes to Japan. I really enjoy traveling to Japan because it's so different from the West.

My first trip to Japan was with Roberta Flack. Then I went back over several times with John Hicks, the pianist. I traveled there with David Murray, the saxophone player. And I was there several times with other musicians. My last trip there was with Dr. Lonnie Smith and the James Brown horn players—Fred Wesley, Bootsy Collins, Maceo Parker and them—and the guitarist Rodney Jones.

I owe a lot of debt and gratitude to Rodney Jones because I got sick there and he helped me out a lot. But I have always enjoyed Japan and it's always been something to look forward to, just going to Japan. The people know who I am and they know my music. I was impressed with how they know all about me over there. And their customs made an impression on me as well. It's like another world there.

The customs is much different. It's actually being in another world. The respect they have for one another: the respect between the man and the woman—the women kind of walking behind the men, whereas here we walk side by side. So they demonstrate great respect and I respect and enjoy that.

When we got off the plane in Japan, the people who pick me up for the John Scofield tour have this "Groove Elation" record playing in the car. I can hear these two different snare drums in their stereo sound system.

I was surprised that I played so great. I mean, it was like shocking. Did I play that? Listen at that. It was real slick. You could hear it so well on the record. Most of the records that I make for people, I might listen to them once or twice. That's it. I don't want to get caught up or trapped inside of it.

I think this was a great band for John Scofield. I enjoyed playing with Larry Goldings and Dennis Irwin too. I think John is one of the innovators of modern guitar playing today. Thinking back on when I first met and played with John, coming out of the "Turn This Mutha Out" tour, that's what made me determine it would be more profitable to work as a sideman. I can help other people, demand a "leader's fee" for myself, and avoid the headaches. It would be like the old days in New York.

So I might be in Chicago at Joe Segal's Jazz Showcase with John Scofield; then back on the very same stage three weeks later with Joe Lovano or the Ahmad Jamal trio. Sometimes one band isn't enough to keep me as busy, working all the time, as I like to be.

Black Jeans

In my early days of living in New York, musicians were eager to learn things, they were eager to show you how to do something. And the ones who were working, they were sharp. They were clean. Even when they weren't working, they were sharp.

And this situation now, as I see the cats, everybody wears jeans. Even to go to work, cats wear black jeans and a coat and a shirt. You see a cat in a club, he look like just came from out of the garbage can. You couldn't get on the bandstand like that, man—back in those days.

You had to have a suit—a full suit, white shirt and a tie. Plus, the music was different. The music was much, much, much different.

You hear bands playing today, the compositions that they have written, and the music doesn't come compared to the sound of music that we had then. We had a lot of songs written at that time. Today musicians who write their own music don't have time to put any feeling to it, some of them.

You have these cats selling a million records in the first weeks' time. Do you have any idea how much money that is? A million seller? In the first week that this record is out? Sure these cats open up their own clothes line, house on both coasts, they've got a Bentley. They've got so much money they've got to put it in *something*.

I mean, it was the same back then. We didn't make the kind of money they make now, but it was equivalent to it. Alan Toussaint was riding around in a Rolls Royce, getting suits made the same color as the car—silk suits. Fats Domino, Larry Williams, Jerry Butler and them bought a new Cadillac every year.

I'm laughing but, man, I always wanted a Rolls Royce. I would have had a Rolls Royce too, had I not played jazz. I think the jazz slowed me down.

And also, *everybody* is a star now. Because they get one record deal and they're mister big stuff. But they can't play shit. Some of them can't play three good notes and one chorus of music. Then they got the other ones that play too many notes. That quality is the difference of the guys who have been in the music business and still can play.

Like Ahmad Jamal. Ain't but one can do that. Many piano players, many piano players, but they don't come up to the standard of Ahmad.

Piano Black

I'm going to tell you about my experience playing with three unique pianists. I have played with many, many piano players, but this will give you an idea about three of them, how that came about and how I like to work. The three pianists are Ahmad Jamal, Randy Weston and John Hicks.

I met Ahmad Jamal in 1960 when he opened The Alhambra club in Chicago on the success of the hit record, "Poinciana." I've been knowing Ahmad for a very long time—more than 50 years. He was the best man at my wedding to Sakinah—LaLa Brooks.

When I was in Austria in the mid-1990s, I got the phone call. It's Ahmad. He says he wants me to come to Paris and make a record. I went to Paris. I made the record. The record was great. But I am too busy to work with him because I have too much stuff going on. I'm doing great, working with James Moody, Joe Lovano and all of them. But Ahmad offers to pay me a lot of money—a lot of money, man.

I'm going to discuss Ahmad more thoroughly last in this comparison. But I have been knowing him the longest and have been playing with him the most recently.

I had done a very successful series of record dates around 1991 with the pianist Randy Weston. We had a week to do three albums. And we did them in three days! We did one about Thelonious Monk, another was the music of Duke Ellington and the third album was Randy Weston's original music called "African Sunrise." We did those three records in three days. That put Randy Weston back on the map. He had been living and working in Morocco for about 20 years. Randy hadn't done a record in the States for a while.

They sent for me and Jamil Nasser to go through to Paris to do these records with him. So we did three records for him in three days because it went that fast. We ended up doing a record per day. We knew how to record and make records. So we explained to Randy Weston that most of the stuff we're doing, we just do it and take the first take.

It came out real great for Randy because he it put him back on the map, because he had been away for twenty years. Those records that I did for him and put him on the map were recorded in Paris. I was able to do a couple of tours with him and then he started touring with just the percussion player.

I had set the bar so high, he didn't hire no more drums—he just hired percussion players. He hired a guy who I had worked with before named Big Black. I enjoy working with Big Black because he's not a show-off. He is a good player and I like him because he was very calm. It is easy to play with him. As a rule, though, percussion players always get in the way. Before I did the records for Randy Weston, though, I played a lot with John Hicks. I'll tell you some about John Hicks.

I met John Hicks in New York in the 1960s. We were doing a gig with the saxophone player Lucky Thompson. I actually knew John Hicks even before all this. But I didn't play with him. I just knew him. This was before the Pharoah Sanders period because the first record John Hicks and I did was with Lucky Thompson. Early days. John Hicks and I made a gig with Lucky Thompson and we made a record too. The record was done in New York.

The gig after Lucky Thompson was with Betty Carter. Rather than use Lucky Thompson, Betty Carter needed George Coleman. So the band was George Coleman on saxophone, John Hicks on piano, Paul Chambers on bass and myself, that was Betty Carter's band. Our first gig was at the Five Spot.

This was when I was working in the Apollo Theater's band. And we would play at the Five Spot sometimes. The guys heard me play; they thought I was a jazz guy but I wasn't. So one night Betty Carter heard me playing at the Five Spot and she asked me to do a gig with her. And our first gig was also at the Five Spot.

It's funny how this came about. There was a piano player named Walter Davis, Jr. He had actually booked this particular gig at the Five Spot but he didn't book it with Betty Carter, he booked it with his wife. When his wife couldn't make the gig, she wouldn't let Walter Davis play with Betty Carter. So Betty Carter took the gig and brought in George Coleman, Paul Chambers and me. And I brought in John Hicks to replace Walter Davis, Jr.

We played in New York, Philadelphia—all around. We made a record with Betty and we worked with her for a while. It ended because I got a job in "Hair." That's how it ended for me. John kept playing with her though.

Everybody knew everybody in New York. Whoever was playing and was a great player, everybody knew you. The grapevine is everything that went down in New York. And everybody heard about it and talked about it. So the word got out. That's how the grapevine worked in New York.

The grapevine is how I started working with Pharoah Sanders in the late 1960s. This was after I had left Betty Carter's band but during the period, initially at least, when I was still doing "Hair" on Broadway. I had been playing in John Hick's trio. I met Pharoah at Slugs in New York. We made about ten records together, something like that, John Hicks and I did with Pharoah.

But the group broke up because there were three leaders. John Hicks, Pharoah Sander and myself. So that was a way out to leave, because a band can only have one leader. And we all were recording, we all was doing individual recordings, we all had our own records out. But it was through playing together like we did before it ended that the Keystone Trio was forged.

The Keystone is a club in San Francisco. Todd Barkan owned that club. And the Keystone club was just across the street from a police station. It was John Hicks, Curtis Lundy on bass and myself—that was the Keystone Trio. And I made a lot of records with John Hicks as the Keystone Trio.

And now let's fast forward to the last records I did with Ahmad Jamal. But in contrasting and comparing the three pianists—there is no comparison. It was three different guys. Out of the three piano players, I liked John Hicks. I liked him best. He was easier and more fun to play with. I enjoyed it more.

I did about half a dozen records with Ahmad Jamal The last record I did with Ahmad followed the series of three albums called "The Essence." The difference between the series of three records of "The Essence" series and the three records I did with Randy Weston is that the records I did with Randy Weston were done in three days total. Then I only toured with Randy a little bit because I was so busy. With John Hicks, we performed and we billed as equals because we both were leaders. We played with Betty Carter and Pharoah Sanders together, but also as the Keystone Trio. But the deal with Ahmad is that he hired me to do the records and tour with him as the leader.

When we got to the third record, being "The Essence, Part III," Ahmad hired this percussionist guy that used to work with him. That didn't work out with me too hot. We're back to the same problem.

I don't like percussion players. They get in the way. It seems like every time I get ready to playing something good, they get to banging some shit. I can't play good with percussion players. The only guy I can play with who always comes in and does his stuff right is Ralph MacDonald. Ralph MacDonald is the only percussionist I know that I really enjoy playing with because he isn't a guy that gets in the way. So I'm not too keen with percussion players.

But over the years—way back before I got the call in Austria that day—people kept telling Ahmad, "You've got to get Idris to play with you." We always said we're going to play together. Now we're playing together. In fact, Ahmad is relying on me so much now that he can't play with anyone else.

So when somebody else plays with you, another drummer, you're going to know that I played your music. You're going to turn around and look around and say, "Oh yeah, that ain't Idris." But I don't like that. I don't like the idea of being locked down. Sometimes I like to hear a horn or something. So then I would play with Joe Lovano.

Ahmad is very difficult to play with. Not difficult as far as musicianship, But his dynamics are so fast and so precise and so demanding. He's giving me cues and he's talking to me at the same time. He's giving us cues, he's telling us: this is the top, come down, go up.

Ahmad's music is true music: dynamics, rhythm, harmony, melody all in one. That's why I like to work with him. Because I know what he's about and I can play the shit out of his music.

I know what other guys are about and I can play with them too. My problem is that I play so damn good that once I learn your music I might play it better than you do. And that's a God's gift. That's a gift that I've got. I play with somebody, I'll learn your music, I'll know your music—you might forget some shit, I'll play it for you. But I don't dwell on that when I'm playing your music.

The Ahmad Jamal trio includes James Cammack on bass. James has been with Ahmad for over twenty-five years now. And this trio is globetrotters, man. We've traveled the globe many, many times. We've covered over thirty countries together!

When we did a tour in Japan in 2008 we hit some especially bad weather in the air. Sitting in the front of the plane, flying through this storm, there's the rain and there's the lightning. When something happens to the plane you can feel it. The plane was shivering, man. The pilot came on and said we had been hit by lightning. Then we got hit by lightning again. So we was hit twice by lightning.

That was a sign to me that the Creator up in the sky runs everything. Down here too, but he's really running things up there. He's the one who gives permission for everything to happen. So it helps to make a human being realize that there is a power stronger than the human power.

Another tour with Ahmad and James that stands out is when we played the Middle East. We traveled into Istanbul, Turkey, where they make great cymbals. This is when I got my cymbal endorsement with Istanbul Agop Cymbals.

Istanbul Agop Cymbals

I walk into the factory in a white suit. There's black smoke and soot everywhere. The guys are all rolling up my suit sleeves and pant legs so I won't get ruined from it and we take a walk downstairs.

It's black smoke and it's hot as hell down there. The cats are sweating their asses off. There are four floors at the factory. Each floor is basically one big room where a specific process is executed. The actual Istanbul Agop Cymbal making process as well as the formula is still a secret. Because they hand-make my cymbals for me I got to tour the Istanbul cymbal factory in Turkey.

In the first room is the basement. There's a wood stove, the cookers, and the wood from the cookers, which smoke the metal. They put gold inside the cymbals from back in the old days. There are gold wires that run underground in Turkey which connected the telephone system. In order for the system to last they had to use gold. They would dig up the old wires and mix that gold in with copper and tin.

That's what my signature line cymbals are made from. They're comprised of strands of these three metals braided together. They pour the three metals into the molds. And then they cook it in the ovens like you cook bread or pizza. When they pull the square cymbal plates out, they look like they're covered in black soot.

In the next room is the guy who presses the bell into the square piece. They have four pounders, four of them guys sitting around on the floor hitting the plates with an iron hammer. There's a round iron piece under the plate where they hit it with the hammer. It sounds just like guys are making horseshoes.

These are the guys who put the hammer beats in them. The 22 inch cymbals have 4,500 hammer beats in them. The 20 inch cymbals have 3,000 hammer beats. And so forth.

In the third room awaits the cutter. The cutter cuts the top layer off of it. That's the beginning of seeing what looks like an actual cymbal. Then he sends it to an edger to have the edges trimmed off. Then they cut the grooves into them. When the cymbal is complete, the bottom isn't finished. We leave the bottoms unfinished on my signature line, meaning they don't cut the grooves into the bottoms.

In the final room is the polisher. Then they paint the logos on them. I saw the whole process. And that's the making of a cymbal. Plus they gave me some cymbal bags.

I was putting each cymbal in a cloth and separating them. They gave me a metal case which works well for me because they make heavy cymbals for me so I can get the sound out of it I like.

I had been with Zildjian, but I didn't like the way they treated me. I saw some things that upset me. When I joined Istanbul Agop Cymbals in Turkey they said they'd give me a full endorsement. They gave me a whole wall of cymbals. I said I couldn't lug those around with me and so they shipped them to me in New York. The guys at Istanbul Agop Cymbals are really cool, man.

Joe Lovano

For some drummers it can feel like they put you in a cage. That's the analogy I use. So I especially like to play with horn players because they can't keep me in a cage, man. I like to strike out and play very free. On the bandstand, I take no prisoners.

All of it, I play your music, play your music, play your music. And I don't flaunt that. I just do it. I'm always thinking of music. Hearing music. Music, music, music, music, music—all the time. Although I might not be playing it, I got music in my head.

Joe Lovano and I work together so much because we are good for each other. We have so much fun and it's so enjoyable to play with each other that we want to do that as much as we can. Originally we had a gig together and it wasn't his gig and it wasn't my gig and out of that we just decided to play together.

When he had his loft on 23rd Street in New York he had a set of drums. Joe's drums is a Gretsch collector's item drum set, an older drum set. Ed Blackwell used to go there a lot. Also Michael Brecker, the saxophone player. Michael Brecker could play the drums. Bob Mintzer, the horn player, he could play the drums too. He used to play in Buddy Rich's band, and he used to write a lot of music for Buddy. And he would play the drums on a lot of the arrangements. Then Buddy would watch Bob and he would pick it right up. There's quite a few horn players that can play the drums. Lou Donaldson is another horn player that could play the drums.

I always liked working with the horn players: Gene Ammons, Sonny Rollins, George Coleman, Sonny Stitt. I had more freedom to play with the horn players because in the beginning of me learning how to play jazz I used to listen a lot to John Coltrane. The way Elvin played with John, it was a free way of playing. So I inherited that.

Playing with the horn player—or any musician—sometimes you can't go past the line because you want them to be up front. When you're playing music you have to play with the musician and the drummer's place is to play with the person, not playing in front of the person unless the drummer is the leader.

Musically, sometimes you play with the person. Sometimes you lead the person. Sometimes you follow. Sometimes I like to follow him because I damn near have ESP and I can meet him at the corner. You can take what he's thinking and play the same thing with him at the same time. This can happen with any band. It all depends on the leader—what he has in his mind of his music.

When Joe Lovano did the two records, "Trio Fascination One" and "Trio Fascination Two," Elvin did one and I did one. I can remember Elvin telling people that I'm the closest thing to him. And it was fun for me because I get to play so free with Joe Lovano and the other the horn players.

Section Eight

Today

The First Chief of the Congo Nation

I'm Big Chief Red, the First Chief of the Congo Nation. I'm in the tribe with Donald Harrison, Jr. Our tribe is called Congo Nation. Donald Harrison is the Big Chief. So when I came into the tribe, Donald made me a chief because he thought that my status as a musician deserved to not just be an Indian but to be a chief. So he made me the First Chief of the Congo Nation. And he is the Big Chief.

Donald Harrison's father was the Indian chief of my neighborhood. As a kid I used to follow him and listen at these tambourines and listen at these songs they sang. What I heard Donald Harrison's dad play, I got these rhythms that I'm playing now. I still play this kind of stuff today.

The Indian tradition of today is that they sew these beaded costumes for one year. They are constructed of only hand beads and feathers so it's a very intricate work. It takes a long time to do. And there are many days of sticking your hands with the needles. I know because I done it myself. Now I'm wearing thimbles because I've stuck myself quite a few times. But I'm a beginner.

I masked for the first time and it was like being a kid again. Putting on this costume, wearing these feathers. I knew this dance because I had watched them dance since I was a kid. But the only thing I had to learn was how to get this rap going.

I think the Indians were the original rappers. Because they would be rapping to each that I'm prettier than you, and I'm so pretty that your mother wouldn't like you. So they would say things like that. And I would hear this. So I'm trying to learn how to get this rap going.

The Indian tribes had some rhythms that they played on the tambourines. This tradition came about in the early days of New Orleans, the French Colonial days. The slaves and the Indians who were there had one day of the year when they didn't have to work. They could just enjoy themselves. So they made this day a festivity day. They just had a ball.

The black slaves would intermingle with the Indians. They would intermingle and they would marry and they would be like that. The blacks on this Mardi Gras day that they made, they would dress up like the Indians. They would put on the costumes; they would dance; and they would sing these songs. So this is where the tradition came from.

Then it developed to where these guys started these different tribes: The Wild Magnolias, The Wild Tchoupitoulas, The Golden Eagles, these are some of the different tribes in New Orleans.

In the beginning, they would dress to see who could out dance each other. Sometimes they had fights, and they had different things, because this tribe was from downtown and this tribe was from uptown. When they met at a certain spot, there's a certain saying: "I'm the spy boy and I don't bow down." That means that when the tribe comes, he won't bow down to you. So he would much rather fight than to get down on his knees to you, so that's how they did.

A Conduit for Music

Inside the vortex, I wasn't mindful of the broad currents of history at work. But right now I have a lot of time to think about it. I look back at the stuff in New Orleans—from the day that I bought my brother's drums, I clocked up well over 50 years playing the drums and making money on the drums. I think about the first marriage when I was eighteen that lasted only a few years. The divorce. And how the next week I was married again. How I've been single only one week since I was eighteen.

I had two families—took care of two families—sent my kids to private schools in Europe because I didn't like the school system in the United States. I've owned and lived in houses in three countries, the United States, England and Austria.

My thing was about how I can take care of the family, the house, the food. I didn't have time to be talking about how good I am. This attitude kept me where I am. I speak out now because I'm older. I think I've earned the respect of being one of the greatest drummers. So it's my privilege now to speak.

Very few people can do what I do. They do at it, but you can't do what I do. Ain't but one of me. I'm a natural drummer, gifted from the Creator. Gifted. I got gold in my hands. Feet of gold. Perfect precision. Perfect. I will do things that shock me. And then I come home, sit in the tub, and try and figure out how I did this shit. But I don't try and make my mind go back and try and do it again. Because it's a gift that I got from the Creator.

People will say I was the first guy to do this or that. But I wasn't aware of what I had accomplished. I took Paul Barbarin's advice and let it go in one ear and out the other. And now I'm responsible for a whole lot of stuff that's happening today. And you see what else is so amazing: it's that I didn't realize I was a drummer that can play all types of music. I didn't realize how unusual this is.

I'm just a conduit of this music. I realize it doesn't belong to me. A force of energy passes through me and I create this stuff. Because I never flaunted it, never waved the flag, this allowed me to be able to create and remain creative. I never had a halo over me that I was better than anyone else. They would rave about me, but I never took it to heart. I was too busy.

When cats came into my presence that weren't as good as me, I never played them down. I'd say, listen to that shit you are playing, man. I like what you do. Cats would say, man, show me how to play this beat. And I'd take them to the drums and I'd show them how to do this. I always kept a mutual friendship with other drummers. I was humble, humble, humble.

I often saw other drummers standing in the wings watching me. Sometimes when we didn't have anything to do between shows we'd play the drums. Some of them could play it. Some of them took some of it and went with it. But every night I played something different. Every night I didn't play the same stuff.

I don't hear it when people praise me because I need that energy that flows through me to keep coming through. It's special. It's a direction of energy that flows through us all. It's a magical thing that comes from the Creator.

I'm happy that I was able to create something these other people—especially the guys coming up under me—can learn from and be successful. It doesn't matter who makes what money. It's not about that. It's about how we can gather these things as human beings. I'll throw something out and the drummers are hearing it—and if they're taking it—if a drummer's successful with it, then it's all up to him. It's not upon me because I am only a conduit of creating music.

I'm a sharer. I like to be friends with people. I like to help people. And when you share with people good things come back around to you. It used to be that I would send my mother some money. And then I would go to the musician's union to pick up some payments that I knew was there for me. But then there was often a check that I didn't know was there. Or then I might get a gig that paid a whole lot of money!

When I work with people they become often successful. And when I leave them they are on top. All of the people that I've worked for, when I left them they were successful.

It's about how we can gather these things as human beings. I learned how to treat others as human beings. I kept a dignified rapport with people and an attitude which in turn made me a lot of money; it made me a lot of friends; it made me make a lot of history. Just that rapport and that attitude did that.

I hope that the records that I done for the people who I did it for, I hope that—some of them are gone, some of them are here—that they're happy with this work. I knew when I did the date, the guys always was happy. When I left the record date, the people was always happy with my work. Some guys were very fortunate. Bob James, Grover Washington, George Benson and a lot of other guys were really successful in the music industry and it's great. And they know me and they acknowledge this fact to me, that I was a part of their life being a success.

Now I might be just sitting by the window in upstate New York watching the snow come down. I'm watching the television. The television is watching me. I have a home near where the Alfred Hitchcock mansion is located. Timothy Leary and all them used to hang out up here. They used to drop acid and wander around the horse barn and out into the yard that surrounds my home.

Or I might be in New Orleans because I have homes in both New York and New Orleans. I spent most of my life in New York and New Orleans. They are a part of me. And I'm a part of them, musically.

Cats are asking me to play the drums down in New Orleans. But don't ask me to travel again. You would have to send a Lear Jet to get me out of New Orleans. Meanwhile, the Ninth Ward was taken out by Katrina, and the people are building their houses as they did when I was a kid and living in the Thirteen Ward with the Nevilles.

I'm just relaxing. I am just enjoying myself. I always said I was going to get a fishing pole, smoke Cuban cigars and drink Diet Coke. I want now to relax and enjoy my family.

20086922R00131

Printed in Great Britain
by Amazon